The Illustrated Collector's Guide To

KATE BUSH

2nd Edition **Robert Godwin**

PRINTED IN CANADA

 We acknowledge the financial support of the Government of Canada through the Book Publishing Industry Development Program for our publishing activities.

Published by Collectors Guide Ltd, Burlington, Ontario, Canada, L7R 2B5
Printed and bound in Canada

The Collectors Guide to Kate Bush (2nd Edition)/Robert Godwin
ISBN 1-894959-45-0

Front cover by Geoff Godwin
Images courtesy EMI Music

INTRODUCTION (1991)

First I have to put "The Kick Inside" on my CD player and then I can approach this introduction with confidence, (although the word trepidation still springs to mind). I have spent the better part of the last six months reading back issues of "Homeground", "Under The Ivy", "Still Breathing" (to name a few), and I cannot help but feel a little like Daniel (perhaps I should start a fanzine and call it "Lion's Den"). I should perhaps qualify why I feel this way.

Anyone reading this almost certainly doesn't need me to tell them the story of Kate's meteoric rise to prominence on the world stage, it is a story which has been told many times before and that is not the purpose of this book. I have, however, seen the reviews afforded to some of those other books and, thus, my empathy for that biblical hero.

Kate Bush - The adjectives used to describe her in the past are abundant. I would like to use only one which comes to my mind, unique. There is certainly no one in contemporary music who deserves to be called unique more than Kate Bush. There are plenty of female rock\pop singers today, a lot more than when Kate first hit the scene, but when you compare them to Kate Bush they are all easily categorised. Indeed, comparing anyone to Kate seems almost ludicrous.

My first exposure to Kate's incantations was on a British TV appearance, on 16th February 1978. It was Kate's first performance on Top Of The Pops. My recollections are a little fuzzy after all this time but I do remember Kate's bizarre performance (I call it bizarre because that is how it seemed at the time). I am not noted for my ability to recognise budding genius and so I dismissed the whole thing as 'cute' or 'interesting'. The next time I saw her I was tuned into a new show called "Revolver". She had already been to the top of the charts around the world and only a few Buddhist monks in Tibet hadn't heard of her. I didn't even know that Kate was to be featured, and so when she was introduced as "Basil Brush's younger sister" who had the hit "Withering Tights" I was pleasantly surprised. (I forgave Peter Cook for his unflattering joke I had been a fan from the days when he was with Dudley Moore). Kate's fervid interpretation of "Them Heavy People" convinced me that there was something special going on.

Fourteen years later, I feel sorry for the people who haven't shared in the enjoyment that Kate has brought to so many. At this writing she has yet to really make it out of the realms of cult status in the USA, although the dedication of that cult following borders on rabid. She is an icon in Canada, Japan, all over Europe including what was the Eastern Bloc, Brazil, Argentina, and Australia. Not bad. In fact you may be surprised to find mention in these pages of Zimbabwe, Chile, Israel and more.

I find it hard to be objective and to resist the temptation to fill the page with drooling sentiments. Well, why not? Maybe a few.

To me Kate's music is a blend which captures the best elements of Pink Floyd, Peter Gabriel, & Roy Harper, to name the obvious ones. She has the chameleon talents of David Bowie and yet is still able to exude the sincerity of a true disciple, a believer in herself and in her unique amalgam of doctrines.

Forgive me if I offend anyone with my name dropping, but I do so with the knowledge that these are artists who have impressed me with their ingenuity and dedication to their own personal visions. In fourteen years Kate has never compromised her vision, (at least that is the way

I see it) and her ingenuity seems to be boundless.

Contained in the pages of this book you will find no opinions about the music, and no gossip about the artist. This is essentially a text of data. I have been criticized in the past for my clinical approach. I want to stress that it is not for want of opinions that I exclude them. This book is simply not about opinions, it is about facts. You will find in these pages an incredible array of collectibles which are testament in themselves to an incredible talent.

I have no doubt that there are umpteen collectibles which I have omitted, and probably some mistakes, but I will always be grateful to hear from you, the reader, about them.

I would like to take an opportunity to thank whoever it was at EMI who became the exception to the rule and showed the foresight to give Kate Bush room to breathe. I would like to thank Dave Gilmour for consistently proving his musical genius and for giving Kate a break. Thanks also to the incredible EMI studio musicians who have given us so many amazing performances. My wife Pat, and Dayne and Emily for their patience. Tom Richards at C Side Records who provided 90% of the rare material in these pages (where are you Tom?). Thanks to Paul Evans for filling some gaps. Once again thanks to Gilles Lefranc for providing the stuff that didn't exist, and Bob Walker for his untiring support.

And to Kate please be kind to *my* mistakes.

Robert Godwin
Burlington Fall 1991

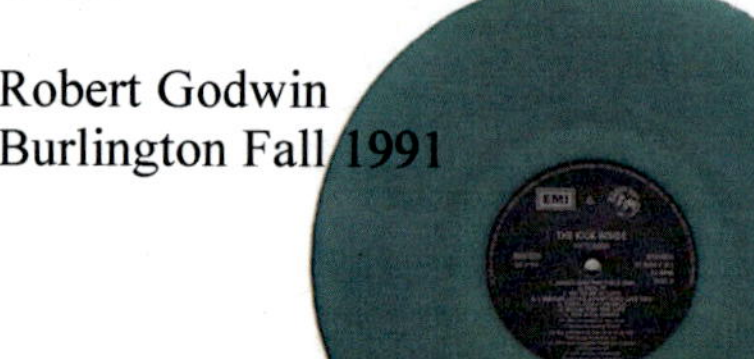

INTRODUCTION (2005)

What can I say? It's been almost a generation since the one and only previous edition of this book. My kids are grown up and I'm still a Kate Bush geek. It's been a long drought for the dedicated Kate Bush enthusiast. I don't know if I can think of any other major contemporary artist that could drop recording and performing for over a decade and then create the kind of buzz that surrounds *Aerial*. Once again Kate confounds and astounds and comes back with a double album. Since the first edition of this humble guide there have been two major releases by Kate, *The Red Shoes* and *Aerial*. However there have been innumerable other things that have quietly slipped out into the market (over 100). Several singles from Red Shoes, a pile of promos, a bunch of bootlegs and of course we discovered a little thing called the Internet. Now we have many, many Kate Bush websites which have all but replaced the fanzines. Since my last attempt at a book like this I've been the recipient of many nice letters from people giving me details of the stuff I missed last time. Needless to say any book of this kind can't possibly be comprehensive but it is kind of fun to have many of the facts in one place and the last time I checked it's still difficult for most of us to take websites to the record shows. Anyway, I hope you find the book to be more presentable than last time (cut and paste has a whole new meaning since then) and I trust you will all continue to support your favourite artist even if it is another fourteen years before the next edition of this book. Buy these records!

Special thanks to Eugene Guest for the Australian stuff, G'day mate. And to EMI for cover pics.

Rob Godwin
Burlington Fall 2005

VINYL ALBUMS

THE KICK INSIDE

Kate's first album released in the UK on 17th February 1978. This album was commercially available around the world and was packaged with several notable cover variations. The back cover was essentially the same everywhere, however the front cover was completely different in Canada, the United States, Argentina, Japan, Yugoslavia and Uruguay, amongst others. There were also two pressings in the UK as a picture disc. The reported quantities for each pressing vary considerably. The original picture disc had a circular sticker on the cover, on the reissue it was oval.

Cassette - E446012

LP
SW11761 (Orig US)
SW17003 (US re-issue with diff. cover)
N 46012 (Canada, portrait cover)
EMC 3223 (UK, New Zealand)
EMPC 3223(UK Picture disc)
EMS 81042 (Japan)
EMS 63026 (Japan)
FA 3207 (UK re issue)
SC062 06603 (Holland Grey Vinyl)
EMI SLPE 500.750 (Uruguay)
LSEMI 70870 (Yugoslavia)
Portrait CBS EMC 3223 (Israel)
Pathe PM 251 (France)
EMI 6858 (Argentina)
EMI 064 06 603 (Germany)
EMI 062 006.603 (Spain)
EMI 3223 (Australia)
EMI SLEM-795 (Mexico)
EMI/Globus 210093-1 311 (Czech) on green, pink and multi colored vinyl

UK

USA

Can

UK

Czech.

Spain

UK

Arg.

UK

UK

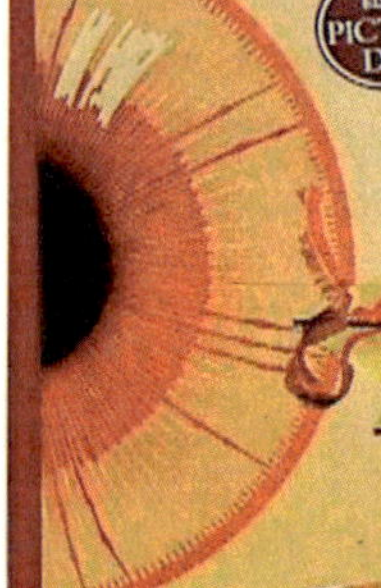

Urg.

Yug.

Japan

LIONHEART

This swift follow up album was assembled from the huge backlog of original songs that Kate brought to EMI when she first signed. Released in the UK on 10th November 1978. The first versions had the title embossed into the cover, this was temporarily dropped and then reintroduced. The Japanese version has a nice variation to the traditional wrap around paper price band. It is printed with the appropriate part of the cover picture so it does not obscure the art, it is however not a gatefold, but instead has the internal artwork printed onto the dust jacket. There is also the obligatory Japanese lyric sheet. There has been much speculation as to whether this album was ever released in the USA in 1979: illustrated is the green label of the original. When it did finally see a *substantial* US release in 1984 it was in a single pocket jacket. It was released in Canada in the full gatefold jacket with the embossed lettering on the Harvest label.

UK

Ger.

Japan

Arg.

LP
EMA 787 (UK)
STAO6456 (Canada)
N46065 (Canada)
SMAS 17008 (Green Label 1979 US)
SMAS 17008 (US)
FA 4130941 (UK re issue)
EMS 81135 (Japan)
062 06859 (Holland)
SP261 (France Sonopresse)
PM 261 (France)
EMI 8582 (Argentina)
ATR LP008 (Germany Half speed)
EMA 787 (Australia)
EMA 787 (Malaysia)

Cassette
E446065
(Fame)4130944 (UK)

UK

Arg.

Bul.

Japan

Bul.

NEVER FOR EVER

Released 8th September 1980 in the UK. The original pressing had four colour labels on the disc which featured Kate dressed in the famous bat costume and in the swan costume later featured in the Delius video (shown on BBC TV's Dr Hook show on 7th April 1980.) The original Canadian pressing was again on Harvest records. This album was bypassed by the US division of Capitol EMI until 1984, when it was released in a single pocket jacket. It was also pressed in 1990 in Bulgaria on Balkanton records with a single pocket cover (left). This was undoubtedly done to cash in on the Trio Bulgarka's involvement with Kate on the Sensual World album.

Cassette
E446360

LP
ST17115 (US)
STAO6476 (Canada)
N 46360 (Canada)
EMA794 (UK)
EMS 81336 (Japan)
BTA 12540 (Bulgaria)
Yugoton LSEMI78026 (Yugoslavia)
EMI 8934 (Argentina)
EMS 81336 (Japan)
EMA 794 (Australia)
EMI 11819 (Colombia)

THE DREAMING

Originally released in the UK on 13th September 1982. This was the first album since The Kick Inside that enjoyed a full US release on schedule,where it then charted in the Billboard top 200. The original Canadian pressing came with the lyrics printed onto a thin plastic dust sleeve, and with picture labels that were much darker than their British counterparts. The lyric dust jacket in the UK was a more conventional cardboard affair. The US release was accompanied by a larger selection of promo items than had been normal previously (see section on promos).

Cassette
E446361 (US & Canada)

LP
ST17084 (US & Canada)
ST 17084 (US on coloured vinyl only five copies)
EMC 3419 (UK)
N46361 (Canada)
EMS 91044 (Japan)
EMC 3419 (Australia)(with and without lyric sheet)
EMI 3C064-64589 (Italy)

HOUNDS OF LOVE

Released in the UK 16th September 1985. Three years in the making and greeted with enormous enthusiasm from the press. Once again EMI America put a big promo push behind this record, consequently the first pressings in the USA were on limited 'Marbleized' vinyl. A cute way of describing an incredibly ugly mixture of black and white vinyl. Capitol EMI Canada, which had already established a reputation for making interesting coloured vinyl of Kate, released their first pressings on a mixture of pink and white which produced a much more attractive end prod-

USA

Japan

GDR

uct. The Canadian version is harder to find. A similar mix of pink and white plastic was used for the cassette shells in Canada. The original British cassette and the Canadian marbled shell also featured the extended re mix of Running Up That Hill. This was the first album by Kate to have the CD released simultaneously with the LP.

Cassette
E446164 (USA) -
17171 4 (USA) marble shell
4XT17171 (Pink shell Canada with extra 12” mix of RUTH)
TCKAB 1 (UK with extra 12” mix of RUTH)

LP
KAB 1 (UK)
ST17171 (Canada & US)
EMI Odeon 2403841 (Spain)
EMCJD 2403841 (Zimbabwe)
EMI 8344 (Argentina)
EMS 91113 (Japan)
EMA 240384 (Australia)
EMI 240 3841 (Philippines)

KATE BUSH

A curious obscurity, this album was released in 1984 by a record label called “Amiga”. The company name is so prominent on the album cover that some people have misinterpreted it to be the album’s title. Ostensibly manufactured under license from EMI in the German Democratic Republic it is a nicely presented compilation of tracks from the first three albums. Some have speculated that this may have been a pirate album but the overall quality of the package suggests otherwise. Regardless of origin it is quite rare and collectible. At press time no CD version has been seen but the cover lists a matrix number for a cassette version Track listing S1: Babooshka - Delius - Moving - Saxophone Song - Hammer Horror - Wuthering Heights S2: Don’t Push Your Foot On The Heartbrake - The Kick Inside - Violin - The Infant Kiss - Army Dreamers - L’Amour Looks Something Like You
Amiga 856 072 (GDR) LP
Amiga 056 072 (GDR) Cassette

THE WHOLE STORY

UK

First released on 10th November 1986 in the UK. Kate's "Greatest Hits" album. This featured a new version of "Wuthering Heights" with the vocal track re recorded. The only other track which was not previously available on an album was the new single "Experiment IV". Another massive promotional campaign was launched to support this record, with a matching Laserdisc and video tape featuring most of Kate's promotional videos, a songbook, mobiles, and more.

Czech.

Cassette
4WAS17242
TCKBTV1 (UK)
RE2094 (Japan) with wrap around

LP
PWAS17242 (US & Canada) -
KBTV1 (UK)
Opus 91132056 (Czechoslovakia)
(Argentina)
EMC 261201 (Australia)

THE SENSUAL WORLD

UK

First released in the UK on 16th October 1989. Once again accompanied by a wealth of promotion on both sides of the Atlantic. Kate's first album with Columbia records in the USA. The CD and cassette included one extra track which was not on the LP, "Walk Straight Down The Middle". Columbia supported the release with several promotional CD singles, an 8" Laserdisc and video tape release of the promotional videos. In Canada, Capitol EMI pressed the CD as a picture disc, which proved to be a shrewd marketing move as large quantities of this were imported into Europe and the USA. Capitol Canada and EMI UK also followed up with a promo case that featured the CD, a cassette single and some biographical material. Lagging behind, Columbia released a CD EP called "Aspects Of The Sensual World" (pic on page 20). To quote the press kit, the promotion for this release in Canada was as follows; Press Conference in London, Deluxe Press Package with CD and tape, open ended video interview,

UK

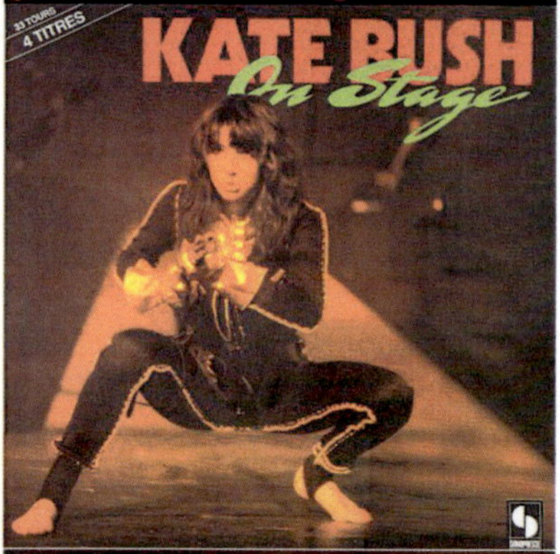

Fra.

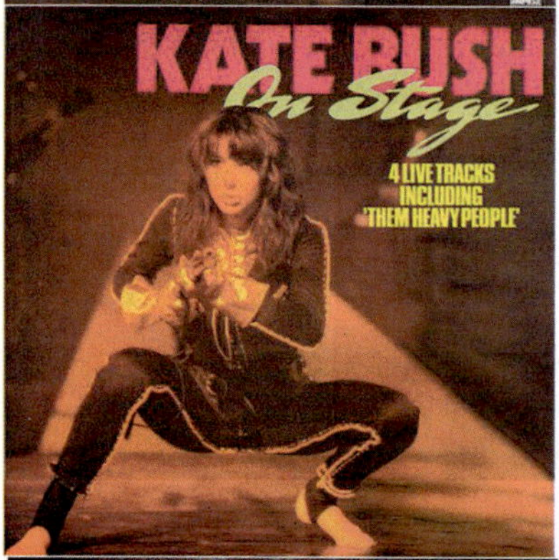

Holl.

limited edition CD singles for giveaways, postcard mailing, radio contest, promo videos, full page teaser ads, 13 page teaser style ads, street newspaper campaign, flats, four types of poster.

Cassette
C493078 (Canada)
LP
C193078 (Canada)
EMD 1010 (UK)
CBS OC44164 (US)

12" EP (MINI LP's)

ON STAGE

Them Heavy People - Don't Push Your Foot on the Heartbrake/ James & The Cold Gun - L'Amour Looks Something Like You

Cassette
Harvest 4LP3005 (Canada)
Capitol 4DP3005 (Canada)

12" EP
DLP3005 (Canada)
IAK052Z07133 (Europe)
EMS 10001 (Japan)
Sonopresse 2C06207133 (France)

MINI LP

This mini LP was released only in North America where it came in two incarnations. The Canadian version had six tracks and the US version only had five tracks. The extra track was Ne T'Enfuis Pas. The Canadian version also came in seven different colours of vinyl which are now highly collectible. The colours for the Canadian version were reported to be clear, brown, blue, white, red, green, and black. Sat In Your Lap - James & The Cold Gun/ Babooshka - Suspended in Gaffa - Un Baiser D'Enfant

Cassette
4LP19004 (Canada)

12" EP -
MLP19004 (Canada & US)

THIS WOMAN'S WORK

Can

A box set of Kate's entire catalogue up to and including Sensual World. Released in three different formats in the UK and Canada and one format in Japan. The Canadian pressing was manufactured in the UK and is barely distinguishable from the UK version. The Japanese did not release a vinyl version.

Cassette
79 5237 4 (UK and Canada)

LP
79 5237 1 (UK and Canada

THE RED SHOES

UK

A relatively limited pressing of vinyl versions of the album appeared in 1993, mostly in Europe. North American pressings are not known to exist. It did, however, also appear as a Minidisc in the USA.
EMD1047 LP
MDEMD1047 MD

AERIAL

UK

(Recording released 7th November 2005)
EMI 343 9601 Double Vinyl album (UK)

1. King Of The Mountain, Pi, Bertie, Mrs Bartoluzzi

2. How To Be Invisible, Joanni, A Coral Room

3. Prelude, Prologue, An Architect's Dream, The Painter's Link, Sunset, Aerial Tal

4. Somewhere In Between, Nocturn, Aerial

USA

Japan

UK

UK

COMPACT DISCS

The Kick Inside

(Recording originally released 17th Feb 1978, UK CD released Jan 1984)
EMI CDP 74060122 & Fame CDFA 3207 (UK)
EMI E21Y 46012 - (US)
EMI CP35 3045 & CP21 6082 (Japan)
With lyric booklet in English & Japanese and typo on cover 'Wethering Heights'

Moving (3.01)
The Saxophone Song (3.51)
Strange Phenomena (2.57)
Kite (2.56)
Man With The Child In His Eyes (2.39)
Wuthering Heights (4.28)
James And The Cold Gun (3.34)
Feel It (3.02)
Oh To Be In Love (3.18)
L'Amour Looks Something Like You (2.27)
Them Heavy People (3.04)
Room For The Life (4.03)
The Kick Inside (3.35)

Lionheart

(Recording originally released 10th Nov 1978, UK CD released Jan 1985)
EMI CDP 7460652 & Fame CDFA 3094 (UK)
EMI E21Y 46065 (US)
EMI CP32 5040 & CP21 6083 (Japan)
With lyric sheet in English & Japanese

Symphony In Blue (3.36)
In Search Of Peter Pan (3.46)
Wow (3.58)
Don't Push Your Foot On The Heartbrake (3.12)
Oh England My Lionheart (3.10)
Fullhouse (3.13)
In The Warm Room (3.35)
Kashka From Baghdad (3.55)
Coffee Homeground (3.38)
Hammer Horror (4.39)

Never For Ever

(Recording originally released 8th Sept 1980, UK CD released Mar 1987)

EMI CDP 746360 2 (UK)
EMI E21Y 46360 (US)
EMI CP32 5276 (Japan)

Babooshka (3.20)
Delius (Song Of Summer) (2.51)
Blow Away (3.33)
All We Ever Look For (3.47)
Egypt (4.10)
The Wedding List (4.15)
Violin (3.15)
The Infant Kiss (2.49)
Night Scented Stock (0.51)
Army Dreamers (2.55)
Breathing (5.30)

UK

Japan (Box set)

The Dreaming

(Recording originally released 13th Sept 1982, UK CD released Jan 1987)

EMI CDP 746361 2 (UK)
EMI E21Y 46361 (US)
EMI CP32 5277 (Japan)

Sat In Your Lap (3.29)
There Goes A Tenner (3.26)
Pull Out The Pin (5.26)
Suspended In Gaffa (3.55)
Leave It Open (3.21)
The Dreaming (4.41)
Night Of The Swallow (5.24)
All The Love (4.29)
Houdini (3.50)
Get Out Of My House (5.25)

UK

UK

Hounds Of Love

(Recording originally released 16th Sept 1985, UK CD released Sept 1985)
EMI CDP 746164 2 (UK)
EMI E21Y 46164 (US)
EMI CP32 5086 (Japan)

Running Up That Hill (A Deal With God) (5.03)
Hounds Of Love (3.02)
The Big Sky (4.41)
Mother Stands For Comfort (3.07)
Cloudbusting (5.09)
And Dream Of Sheep (2.45)
Under Ice (2.21)
Waking The Witch (4.18)
Watching You Without Me (4.06)
Jig Of Life (4.04)
Hello Earth (6.12)
The Morning Fog (2.35)

UK

The Hounds Of Love Digitally Remastered

With 6 bonus tracks
EMI CDCNTAV3 / 7243 8 57978 2 8 (UK)

Running Up That Hill (A Deal With God) (5:03)
Hounds Of Love (3:02)
The Big Sky (4:41)
Mother Stands For Comfort (3:07)
Cloudbusting (4:28)
And Dream Of Sheep (2:45)
Under Ice (2:21)
Waking The Witch (4:18)
Watching You Without Me (4:06)
Jig Of Life (4:04)
Hello Earth (6:13)
The Morning Fog (4:04)
The Big Sky (Meteorological Mix)
Running Up That Hill (12" Mix)
Be Kind To My Mistakes
Under The Ivy
Burning Bridge
My Lagan Love

UK

The Whole Story

(Recording originally released 10th Nov 1986, UK CD released Nov 1986) Later released in France as “The Best of Kate Bush”

EMI CDP 746414 2 (UK)
EMI E21Y 46414 - (US)
EMI CP32 5174 (Japan)
EMI 422420 (France)

Wuthering Heights (New Vocal)(4.57)
Cloudbusting (5.09)
The Man With The Child In His Eyes (2.38)
Breathing (5.28)
Wow (3.46)
Hounds Of Love (3.02)
Running Up That Hill (5.00)
Army Dreamers (3.13)
Sat In Your Lap (3.29)
Experiment IV (4.21)
The Dreaming (4.14)
Babooshka (3.29)

Fra.

The Sensual World

(Recording originally released 16th Oct 1989, UK CD released Oct 1989)

EMI CDEMD 1010 (UK) Renumbered CDP 7930782 for box set.
Capitol EMI C2 93078 (Canada) pic disc.
CBS CK 44164 (US)
EMI CP32 5924 (Japan)

The Sensual World (3.57)
Love And Anger (4.39)
The Fog (5.10)
Reaching Out (3.13)
Heads We’re Dancing (5.21)
Deeper Understanding (4.46)
Between A Man And A Woman (3.30)
Never Be Mine (3.40)
Rocket’s Tail (4.08)
This Woman’s Work (3.40)
Walk Straight Down The Middle (4.39)

UK

Can

This Woman’s Work

(Box Set released 22nd Oct 1990)

EMI CDKBBX1 (UK) With photo booklet and stickers
Capitol CDKBBX1 (Canada) With photo booklet and stickers
EMI TOCP 6460 67 (Japan) With photo booklet and biography booklet

Japan

Japan

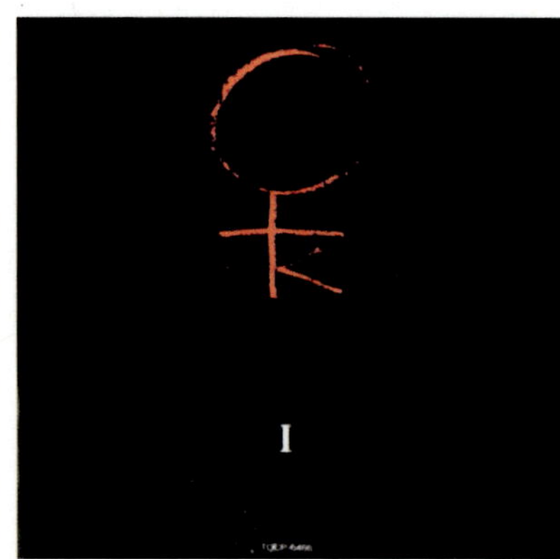

Includes the albums The Kick Inside, Lionheart, Never For Ever, The Dreaming, Hounds Of Love, The Sensual World, and two discs of 'B' sides and remixes as below. All The CD's were packaged with slightly different covers and new serial numbers. The Japanese pressing of "Never For Ever" has an extra front cover which features a close up section of the original artwork. Also included is an extra booklet which tells Kate's day by day track record from 1958-1990, the only drawback is that this nice extra feature is in Japanese. Not released in the United States.

Kate Bush Vol 1.

CDP 7952382 (UK)
TOCP 6466 (Japan)

The Empty Bullring (2.16)
Ran Tan Waltz (2.40)
Passing Through Air (2.03)
December Will Be Magic Again (4.50)
Warm & Soothing (2.43)
Lord Of The Reedy River (2.41)
Ne T'En Fui Pas (2.32)
Un Baiser D'Enfant (3.00)
Under The Ivy (2.09)
Burning Bridge (4.39)
My Lagan Love (2.29)
The Handsome Cabin Boy (3.11)
Not This Time (3.39)
Walk Straight Down The Middle (3.50)
Be Kind To My Mistakes (3.02)

Japan

Kate Bush Vol 2.

CDP 7952392 (UK)
TOCP 6467 (Japan)

I'm Still Waiting (4.28)
Ken(From The Comic Strip Film "GLC") (3.48)
One Last Look Around The House Before We Go (1.02)
Wuthering Heights (New Vocal) (4.57)
Experiment IV (4.21)
Them Heavy People (Live) (4.08)
Don't Push Your Foot On The Heartbrake (Live) (3.39)
James & the Cold Gun (Live) (6.25)
L'Amour Looks Something Like You (Live) (2.43)
Running Up That Hill (12" mix) (5.45)
Cloudbusting (The Organon Mix) (6.31)
Hounds Of Love (Alternative) (3.41)
The Big Sky (Meteorological Mix) (7.43)
Experiment IV (12" Mix) (6.36)

Fin.

Kate Bush

EMI 7243-8 28292 2 (Finland)
Compilation of The Dreaming, Hounds of Love and Sensual World

UK

Hounds of Love/ Sensual World

EBX 27 (UK) Double CD

The Red Shoes

(Recording first released 1st November 1993)

EMI CDEMD1047 (UK)
EMI E272438 2727729 (Canada)
Columbia 53737 (US)
Toshiba-EMI TOCP-7947 (Japan)

Several unauthorised special box sets were created. One included a pair of red dancing shoes in a heart shaped box, another came with a T-shirt in a shoe box.

Rubberband Girl (4.45)
And So Is Love (4.18)
Eat the Music (5.11)
Moments of Pleasure (5.17)
The Song Of Solomon (4.28)
Lily (3.53)
The Red Shoes (4.02)
Top Of The City (4.15)
Constellation of the Heart (4.47)
Big Stripey Lie (3.33)
Why Should I Love You? (5.02)
You're The One (5.52)

UK

The Kick Inside/Lionheart

EMI 5431412 (France) 2002 Double CD

Fra.

Lionheart/ The Dreaming

EMI 5823642 (Germany) Double CD

Ger.

Aerial

(Recording released 7th November 2005)

EMI 3439602 (UK)

EMI P26743960 (Canada)

Sony 1C2K97772 (USA)

EMI TOCP-66474 (Japan)

1. A Sea Of Honey

King Of The Mountain, Pi, Bertie, Mrs Bartoluzzi, How To Be Invisible, Joanni, A Coral Room

2. A Sky Of Honey

Prelude, Prologue, An Architect's Dream, The Painter's Link, Sunset, Aerial Tal Somewhere In Between, Nocturn, Aerial

UK

UK

UK

Japan

USA

Live At The Hammersmith Odeon
CD and video of the concert.

SAV 4913063 (UK)
7243 3 91306 3 0 (Canada)

CD Singles & EPS

The Sensual World - The Sensual World (Instr.) - Walk Straight Down The Middle
EMI CDEM 102 2034942 (UK) 5”
EMI Electrola CDP 552 2034943 (Europe) 3”

The Sensual World - Walk Straight Down the Middle
EMI TODP 2110 (Japan) 3” CD single

This Woman’s Work (Single mix) - Be Kind To My Mistakes - I’m Still Waiting
EMI CDEM 119 (UK)
EMI 2036122 (Europe)

Love And Anger - Ken - The Confrontation - One Last Look Around The House Before We Go..
EMI CDEM 134 (UK)
EMI 2037532 (Europe)

Aspects Of The Sensual World
The Sensual World - Be Kind To My Mistakes - I’m Still Waiting - Ken - The Sensual World (Instr.)
Columbia 44K 73174 (USA)

Rocket Man – Candle In The Wind – Candle In The Wind (Instrumental)
Mercury TRICD2 (UK) in gatefold digipak also unofficial package with lithograph out of USA

Rubberband Girl - Rubberband Girl Extended Mix – Big Stripey Lie
EMI CDEM280 (UK) Also unofficially with Baktabak Interview CD CBAK24011
EMI- E25Q 80829 (Canada)
Toshiba-EMI TOCP-8014 (Japan)

Rubberband Girl – Big Stripey Lie
EMI CDEM280 (Holland, Germany) in cardboard sleeve

Eat The Music – Eat The Music 12" version – Big Stripey Lie – Candle In the Wind
Columbia 44K-77165 (USA) Also in unofficial package with lithograph

Moments of Pleasure – Show A Little Devotion – December Will Be Magic Again – Experiment IV
EMI CDEM297 (UK) Also box set with four color pictures CDEMS297

Moments of Pleasure – Home For Christmas
EMI 7243 881093 2 1 (Holland, Germany) with cardboard sleeve

Rubberband Girl – Rubberband Girl Extended Mix – Show A Little Devotion – Home For Christmas
Columbia 44K-77332 (USA)

The Red Shoes – You Want Alchemy – Cloudbusting (Video Mix) – This Woman's Work
EMI CDEMS316 (UK)

Shoedance (The Red Shoes Dance Mix) – The Big Sky – Running Up That Hall 12" version
EMI CDEM316 (UK)

Eat the Music – Eat The Music Extended version – You Want Alchemy – Shoedance
EMI 7243 8 81317 2 (Holland, Germany)
EMI- 8814112 (Australia) Scratch 'n Sniff

UK

UK

UK

UK

UK

UK

UK

UK

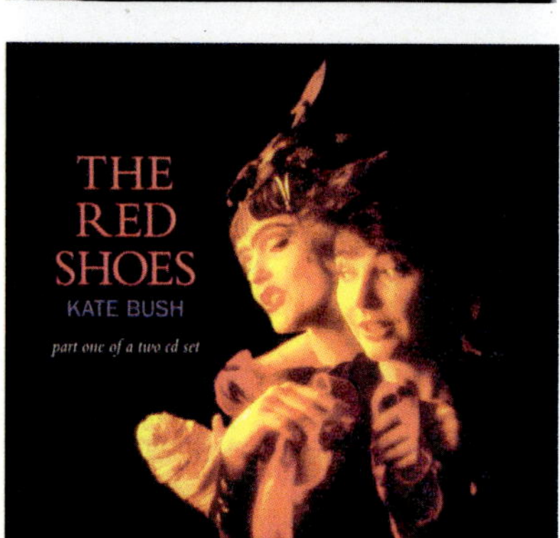

UK

UK

UK

And So Is Love – Rubberband Girl (US) – Eat The Music 12" version
EMI CDEM355 (UK) Also in box with pics

The Man I Love – Rhapsody In Blue – Rhapsody In Blue (edit) (with Larry Adler)
Mercury MERCD 408 (UK)

King Of The Mountain - Sexual Healing
EMI CDEM674 (UK)
Sony IP-6298745 (USA) Download
EMI E21A 45087 (Canada)

CDV and Laserdiscs

Live At Hammersmith Odeon

EMI Music Video SM048 3198 (Japan)
Moving - Them Heavy People - Violin - Strange Phenomena - Hammer Horror - Don't Push Your Foot On The Heartbrake - Wow - Feel It - Kite - James And The Cold Gun - Oh England My Lionheart - Wuthering Heights

The Single File

EMI Picture Music SM058 0019 (Japan)
RCA Columbia 33906 VideoDisc (UK)
Wuthering Heights - The Man With The Child In His Eyes - Hammer Horror - Wow - Them Heavy People - Breathing - Babooshka - Army Dreamers - Sat In Your Lap - The Dreaming - Suspended In Gaffa - There Goes A Tenner

The Hair Of The Hound

EMI Picture Music International SM048 3111 (Japan)
Running Up That Hill - Hounds Of Love - The Big Sky - Cloudbusting

The Whole Story

TOEMI Picture Music International L100 1076 (US) Also 2 disc VideoCD PMCD 4912882 (UK) (next page)
Wuthering Heights - Cloudbusting - The Man With The Child In His Eyes - Breathing - Wow - Hounds Of Love - Running Up That Hill - Army Dreamers - Sat In Your Lap - Experiment IV - The Dreaming - Babooshka - The Big Sky

Japan

Japan

UK

Japan

Japan

UK

USA

Japan

Japan

USA

Japan

The Sensual World Kate Bush The Videos

CMV Image ID7291CB 8" disc with interview and three videos (US)
EMI TOL W-3189 (Japan)
Introduction - Love And Anger - Interlude - The Sensual World - Interlude - This Woman's Work

The Line, The Cross and the Curve

Pioneer PLMPA00901 (UK)
Columbia MLV 50118 (USA)
Toshiba-EMI TOLW3198 (Japan) Pic 204

Peter Gabriel Cv

TOEMI Virgin L050 1115 8 videos featuring Kate on two different versions of 'Don't Give Up' The Big Time - Don't Give Up 2 - Shock The Monkey - Mercy Street - Sledgehammer - I Don't Remember - Red Rain - Don't Give Up 1

VINYL SINGLES

UK

In this section the British singles have been used as a common frame of reference. Most countries followed the British lead and released similar configurations of the 7" format. There are however some notable exceptions when it comes to promos and EP's. One of the most significant developments for collectors of Kate's singles was the advent of "The Single File" box set. Although this is a very attractive and desirable collectible in its own right, it created enormous confusion because dealers were inclined to split it up and try to sell the picture sleeves individually. The high price caused by the demand for the original picture sleeves was one of the reasons that the box set was released, but it inadvertantly gave unscrupulous speculators a chance to clean up by disassembling them. I have attempted to provide a guide to distinguishing the originals from the box set re issues.

USA

THE KICK INSIDE SINGLES

Wuthering Heights/ Kite

The UK original has the printing companies name on the back cover which reads "G & L". The record has an inscription in the dead vinyl run off on side A which reads "Remember The Whales".

Pol.

EMI 2719 (UK)
EMI 8003 (US) Also on gold vinyl
Sonopresse 2S006 06596 (France)
Tonpress S 120 (Poland) Also available with Metallic sleeve
EMI 3C 006 06596 (Italy)
EMI 1C006 06596 (Germany) with mention of Kate's first public
TV appearance on back cover.
EMI C006 006596 (Spain) with three different sleeves

Hol.

Ita.

Ger. (back)

STEREO 1 C 006-06596

Wuthering Heights

Kite

KATE BUSH

Kate Bush
am 9. 2. 1978 in „Bio's Bahnhof"

Obwohl die Talent-Scouts von EMI bereits vor drei Jahren auf sie aufmerksam wurden, bildeten erst die letzten sechs Monate den eigentlichen Start in Kate Bush's Solokarriere. Mit ihren gerade erst 19 Jahren hat die schon äußerlich recht ungewöhnliche Sängerin aus London es immerhin geschafft, eine eigene Band auf die Beine zu stellen und Material für ihr erstes Album zu schreiben – im Februar '78 wird die Langspielplatte unter dem Titel „The Kick Inside" erscheinen. Ihre Gruppe, die KT Bush Band, hat sich in den Pubs und kleineren Hallen in und um London bereits einen ausgezeichneten Ruf erworben – und was Kate Bush's Fähigkeiten als Songschreiberin und Sängerin anbetrifft, so gibt ihre erste Single „Wuthering Heights" darüber schon vielversprechenden Aufschluß.

Wer bereits mit 19 Jahren über einen ausgeprägten Stil und eine so erstaunliche Persönlichkeit verfügt wie Kate Bush, dem sollten in den nächsten Jahren wirklich alle künstlerischen Möglichkeiten offenstehen. Ihre ungewöhnlich hohe Stimme und die tänzerischen Fähigkeiten dürften dabei stets ihre Erkennungszeichen bleiben.

Zusammen mit Produzent Andrew Powell (u. a. Cockney Rebel, Pilot und Allan Parsons) und so versierten Musikern wie Duncan Mackay und Stuart Elliot (von Cockney Rebel) und David Paton und Ian Bairnson (von Pilot) war sie kürzlich im Studio, um ihr erstes Album einzuspielen. Am 9. Februar '78 wird sie beim WDR in Köln erwartet, wo sie in der ersten Sendung von „Bio's Bahnhof" ihr Deutschland-Debut geben wird.

„Wuthering Heights" / „Kite" – EMI 1C 006-06596

ELECTROLA

Spa.

Spa.

Spa.

EMI 006 06596 (Belgium)
EMI 5C006 06596 (Holland) with unique back cover -
EMI 8E 006 06 596 (Portugal) with unique back cover
EMI 1600A B (Argentina)
EMI 1403 2719 (Chile)
EMI 2719 (Sweden) with unique cover and UK pressing of disc
EMI 4589 (Canada)
EMI 11678 (Australia)

The Man With the Child In His Eyes(Single mix)/ Moving

The UK original has the printing company's name on the back cover which reads " G & L". The record has an inscription in the dead vinyl run off on side A which reads "The child hides in the light". The box set reissue shows evidence of the "G & L" having been scratched out and there is also evidence of glue stains in the top rear right hand corner where the promo sticker was on the copy that was shot for re printing.
EMI 2806 (UK)
Sonopresse 2S008 06712 (France)
EMI 1C006 06712 (Germany)
Tonpress S 171 (Poland) with video mix of Man With The Child
EMI 11743 (Australia)
EMI 4C 006 06712 (Belgium)
EMI E 006 06712 (Portugal)
EMI 006 06712 (Holland)
EMI 11743 (Australia)

Wuthering Heights/ The Man With The Child In His Eyes
WMI Old Gold OG 9380 (UK)

Them Heavy People/ The Man With The Child In His Eyes
EMI EMR 20490 (Japan)

Moving/ Wuthering Heights
EMI EMR 20417 (Japan)

4 Successos
Wuthering Heights - Man With The Child In His Eyes / Moving - Oh To Be In Love
EMI 31C 016 06894 (Brazil) EP with picture sleeve

4 Successos
Kate Bush: Wuthering Heights - Harpo: San Franciscan Nights/
Lucifer: Self Pity - Arjan Brass: Leonie
EMI 31C 016 420851 (Brazil) EP with other artists

UK

Pol.

Bel.

Japan

Japan

Bra.

Bra.

UK

THE LIONHEART SINGLES

Hammer Horror/ Coffee Homeground

The UK original cover is very difficult to distinguish from the reissue. The most apparent distinction is in the way that the paper is cut and folded. The fold over flaps on the back of the original have curved corners near to the spine. The reissue has angled corners, also the thumb notch for grasping the record has angular corners, whereas the reissue has curved corners. The original record has the inscription "We are all playing a hunch" on the dead vinyl at the end of side A.

EMI 2887 (UK)
EMI EMR 20530 (Japan)
EMI 11837 (Australia)
EMI 3C 006 06877 (Italy)
EMI C 006 006.877 (Spain)
EMI 4C 006 06877 (Belgium)
(New Zealand)
EMI 006 06877 (Holland)
EMI 11837 (Australia)

Wow/ Fullhouse

The UK original cover is very difficult to distinguish from the reissue. The most apparent distinction is in the way that the paper is cut and folded. The fold over flaps on the back of the original have curved corners near to the spine. The reissue has angled corners, also the thumb notch for grasping the record has angular corners, whereas the reissue has curved corners. The paper used is a heavier stock than on the reissue. The original record has the inscription "Thank you Emily" on the dead vinyl at the end of side A.

EMI 2911 (UK & Ireland))
EMI Harvest 72803 (Canada gold vinyl 2nd pressing has RE 1 in
vinyl run off.

Spa.

Japan

Fra.

UK

Spa.

Can

Fra.

Ger.

EMI 1C 006 06949 (Germany)
EMI 3C 006 07048 (Italy)
Sonopresse 2S 008 06949(France)
EMI 4C 006 6949 (Belgium)
EMI C 006 006.949 (Spain)
EMI E 006 06 949 (Portugal)
EMI 1685 A B (Argentina)
EMI 006 06949 (Holland)
EMI 11897 (Australia)

Symphony In Blue/ Fullhouse
EMI EMR 20567 (Japan) with 'Dolphin' picture sleeve.

Symphony In Blue/ Hammer Horror
Harvest (Canada) 72807 (Blue Vinyl)

Wow/ Symphony In Blue
EMI 3C006 07048 (Italy)

4 Successos
Wow - Hammer Horror / Symphony In Blue - Strange Phenomena
EMI 60.444.436 (Brazil) EP with picture sleeve

Hammer Horror/Oh To Be In Love
EMI 31C 006 06976 (Brazil)

Japan

Can.

Ita.

Bra.

Bra.

NEVER FOR EVER SINGLES

Breathing/ The Empty Bullring

The original UK has a hard cardboard cover which has been UV coated to produce a glossy finish. The original record has the inscription " Happy anniversary to the P's" on side B. Both the original and the reissue have an inscription on side A which reads "We all share the same air".

EMI 5058 (UK)
EMI 1C 006 07286 (Germany) with reversed cover
EMI 2C 008 07286 (France with Bat sleeve)
EMI EMS 17007 (Japan)
EMI 3C006 07286 (Italy)
EMI C006 07 286 (Portugal)
EMI 7C 006 07286 (Sweden)
EMI 006 07286 (Holland)
EMI 249 (Australia)

Babooshka/ Ran Tan Waltz

This one is very difficult to distinguish between the original and the reissue. The thumb notch on the back is cut with angled corners on the original and with a clean curve on the reissue. Also the tip of Kate's bass guitar tends to be obscured by the flap on the back of there issue. These are

UK

Ger.

Fra.

Spa.

Japan

UK

extremely esoteric distinctions which can obviously be faked by unscrupulous dealers. There is no evident difference between the records.

EMI 5085 (UK)
EMI 72838 (Canada)
EMI 2C008 07321 (France) with two different covers
EMS 17047 (Japan)
EMI 31C 006 07321 (Brazil 33RPM)
EMI 298 (Australia)
EMI C006 007.321 (Spain)
EMI C006 007.286 (Spain)
EMI 3C 006 07321 (Italy)
EMI 11C 006 07 321 (Portugal)
EMI 7C 006 07321 (Sweden)
EMI 1 0006 007321 (Germany)
(Argentina)
EMI 1A 006 07321 - (Holland)
EMI 298 (Australia)

Japan

Fra.

Fra.

Spa.

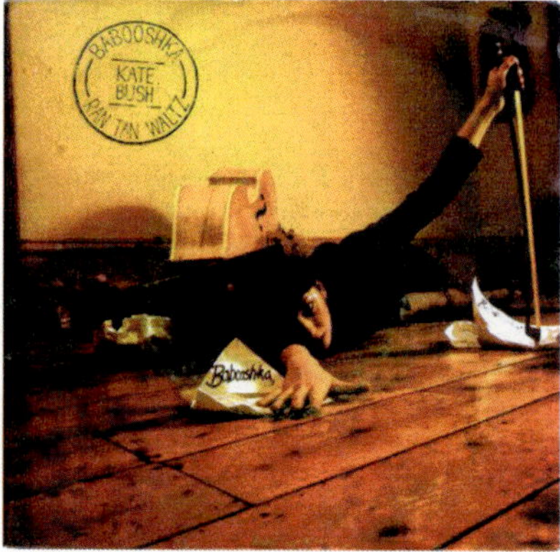

Army Dreamers(Single mix)/ Delius - Passing Through Air

The only way to distinguish the covers between original and re issue with this one is to have the two side by side. The paper is fractionally heavier on the original and the picture is slightly clearer. On the front the original seems to have all four thumb tacks clearly visible, whereas the reissues tend to cut off part of the one in the top left corner. This may not be a consistent feature because of the random nature of paper trimming. The original record has the inscription "Life is to love" on the A side.

EMI 5106 (UK)
EMI 2C 008 07.399 (France)
EMI 006 07399 (Holland)
EMI 394 (Australia)

Army Dreamers / Babooshka
Tonpress S 393 (Poland)

Babooshka
Tonpress R 1074 (Poland) Flexi pic disc with bulls on the disc and flowers on the cover.

4 Successos Vol 4
Kate Bush: Babooshka - Peter Kent: It's A Real Good Feelin'/ Rocky Burnette: Tired Of Toeing The Line - Cliff Richard: Dreamin
EMI 31C 016 420940 (Brazil) EP with other artists

Babooshka
USSR Blue flexi disc with three Doobie Brothers tracks, possibly a pirate. Melodiya T62 09813 14 TY 43 03 48 78

UK

Fra.

Bra.

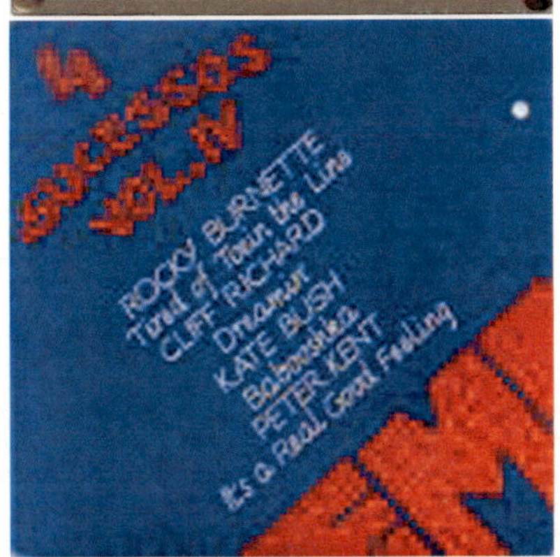

Pol.

USSR

UK

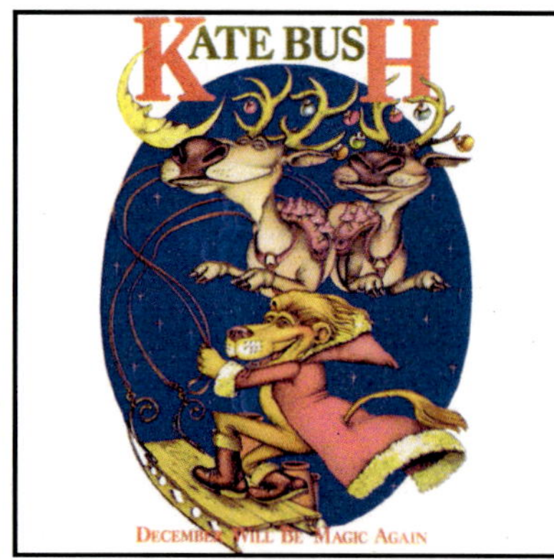

December Will Be Magic Again/ Warm & Soothing

On the original of this one the cover is easy to recognise. Immediately below the credits for side B, on the back cover, are the acknowledgements which read, " Cut by Chris Blair Songs & arrangements by Kate Bush - Cover By Nick Price ". On the reissue these acknowledgements have been split up and spread out across the bottom of the cover in one single line. The inscription on side A of the original is "Happy Christmas".

EMI 5121 (UK)
EMI 1C 006 07421 (Germany) also on green vinyl
EMI 006 07421 (Holland)
EMI 390 (Australia)

UK

THE DREAMING SINGLES

Sat In Your Lap/ Lord Of The Reedy River

Once again the cover of this is so marginally different from the reissue that it is virtually undetectable. The only difference is that the copy is very slightly blurred. Considering the short time frame between the original and the reissue they are probably from the same film. The original record has two inscriptions, side A "Well done JB first Dan" and B side, "Thank You Donovan".

Spa.

EMI 5201 (UK)
EMI 1A 006 64452 (Holland)
EMI 3C 006 64452 (Italy)
EMI C 008 64.452 (France)
EMI 006 064 452 (Spain)
EMI C008 64452 (Portugal)
EMI 540 (Australia)

The Dreaming/ Dreamtime

The original film was almost certainly used to reproduce the cover of the reissue. The only difference is that the black plate was striking in a slightly different place and was also much sharper and clearer on the reissue. Therefore the title type is much sharper and clearer. The original record has the word "TOWNHOUSE" before the EMI matrix number and also has the inscription "For Rolf", presumably a dedication to Mr Harris.

EMI 5296 (UK)
EMI 1C 006 64912 (Germany)
EMI 3C 006 64912 (Italy)
EMI 817 (Australia)
EMI 006 64912 (Holland)
EMI 817 (Australia)

There Goes A Tenner/ Ne T'Enfuis Pas
EMI 5350 (UK)

Suspended In Gaffa/ Dreamtime Instr.
EMI 2C 008 64.957 (France)
EMI 006 064972 (Spain) with There Goes A Tenner sleeve
(Sweden)
EMI 1A006-64972 (Holland)

Suspended In Gaffa/ Ne T'Enfuis Pas
Electrola 006 64972 (Germany)
EMI 905 (Australia)

UK

UK

Fra.

Ger.

Spa.

Hol.

Suspended In Gaffa/ Ne T'Enfuis Pas
EMI 006 64972 (Holland) with mispelled B-side

Un Baiser D'Enfant/ Suspended In Gaffa
EMI 72931 (Canada)
PM 50999 152-7 (France)

Ne T'Enfuis Pas/Dreamtime
Canada EMI 72917

Ne T'Enfuis Pas/ Un Baiser D'Enfant
EMI 5444 (UK)(Released As Part Of The Singles File)
PM 50999 165 152 7 (France)

Night Of The Swallow/ Houdini
Ireland IEMI 9001 with three different sleeve printings. First pressing of the record has IEMI 9001 A on the run off. The second pressing doesn't have the A. The first sleeve has a soft glossy paper sleeve, the second pressing has a hard card sleeve, and the third has a soft matte paper sleeve with a white edge on the left front.

Can.

UK

Ire.

HOUNDS OF LOVE SINGLES

Running Up That Hill/ Under The Ivy
KB1 (UK)
EMI Capitol B8285 (Canada)
EMI America B8285 (US)
EMI EMS 17535 (Japan)
EMI 2007577 (Portugal)
EMI 2007577 (France)
EMI 06 200 7577 (Italy)
EMI 006 2007577 (Spain)
EMI 1553 (Australia)
EMI 006 2007577 (Holland)

Cloudbusting/ Burning Bridge
EMI KB2 (UK)
EMI 062008997 (Italy)
EMI 2008997 (France)
EMI 006 2008997 (Spain)
EMi 006 20 0899 7 (Holland)
EMI 1633 (Australia)

Hounds Of Love/ Handsome Cabin Boy
KB3 (UK) also picture disc KBP 3A.
EMI 1693 (Australia)
(Germany)
EMI 006 20 10577 (Holland)

Hounds Of Love/ Burning Bridge
EMI Capitol B 8302 (Canada & US)
The Big Sky (Single Mix) / Not This Time
KB4 (Also a picture disc KBP 4A) (UK)
EMI Capitol B 72300 (Canada & US)
EMI 1A 006 20 1210 7 (France)
EMI 1794 (Australia)

UK

Japan

UK

UK

Can.

WHOLE STORY SINGLES

UK

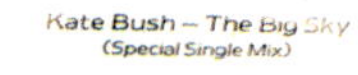

Experiment IV/ Wuthering Heights(New Vocal)
KB5 (UK)
EMI Capitol B8363 (Canada)
EMI EMS 17676 (Japan)
EMI 1886 (Australia)
EMI 201 5337 (France)
EMI 2015337 (Portugal)
EMI J 2015337 (Zimbabwe)
EMI 006 2015337 (Holland)

UK

The Man With The Child In His Eyes/ Sat In Your Lap
EMI B 77014 (Canada)

Wuthering Heights/ Babooshka
EMI Silver Spotlight X 7115 (US)

Cloudbusting/ Man With The Child
EMI B - 8386 (US)

UK

Can.

USA

SENSUAL WORLD SINGLES

UK

The Sensual World/ Walk Straight Down The Middle
EMG 102 (UK) Also picture disc.
EMI Capitol B 73098 (Canada)
Electrola 006 20 34947 (Germany)
PM 102 (France)
EMI 2295 (Australia)

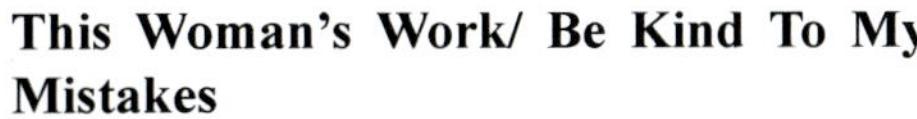

This Woman's Work/ Be Kind To My Mistakes
EMG 119 (UK)
(Also a picture disc EMPD 119)
Electrola 006 2036127 (Germany)
EMI 2341 (Australia)

Love And Anger/ Ken
EMG 134 (UK) With gatefold booklet sleeve.
Electrola 006 2037537 (Germany)
EMI 2384 (Australia)

UK

UK

UK

UK

UK

UK

UK

THE RED SHOES SINGLES

Rubberband Girl – Big Stripey Lie
EMI EM280 (UK)

The Red Shoes – You Want Alchemy
EMI EM316 (UK)

And So Is Love – Rubberband Girl (US)
EMI EMPD355 (UK) Picture Disc with poster

OTHER NOTABLE SINGLES

Kate Bush On Stage

This EP was released in at least four different configurations in the UK. The first was a promo only with two 45 rpm singles with a gatefold sleeve which was folded and glued with no seams showing. It also had no catalogue number on the back right hand corner. The cover was varnished to give a slightly glossy finish, and there was a small sticker placed over the "33 rpm" on the back. The second issue was a single 33 rpm EP in a gatefold cover which was not varnished but was still perfectly bound showing no seams. It also had the serial number MIEP 2991 in the back top right corner. The third issue was a single 33rpm EP in a single pocket cover. The fourth and final issue was in the box set and was a single 33rpm EP in a non glossy gatefold cover which is bound with flaps on the bottom inside with the seams running right through the acknowledgements. You can also see the spine of the original reproduced photographically. The first two EP's are indistinguishable but the box set EP has different labels, the song titles are entirely in capitals on this last version.

UK

EMI MIEP 2991 (UK) 7" EP 33rpm with gatefold sleeve later re issued with single pocket jacket
EMI EP 82000 (Canada) 7" EP in 12" jacket
EMI C 006 007133 (Spain)
EMI 31C 106 17133 (Brazil) 7" EP
EMI 8E 006 07189/90 (Portugal) double 7" set with gatefold sleeve
EMI 016 07133 (Holland) 7" EP
EMI 1C 016 07133 (Germany)

Spa.

Polish Postcards

These unique Polish items are each a laminated picture postcard with a song etched into the laminate on the front. Each card features one KB song. There are at least two companies in Poland making these unlicensed items. The list below is certainly incomplete.

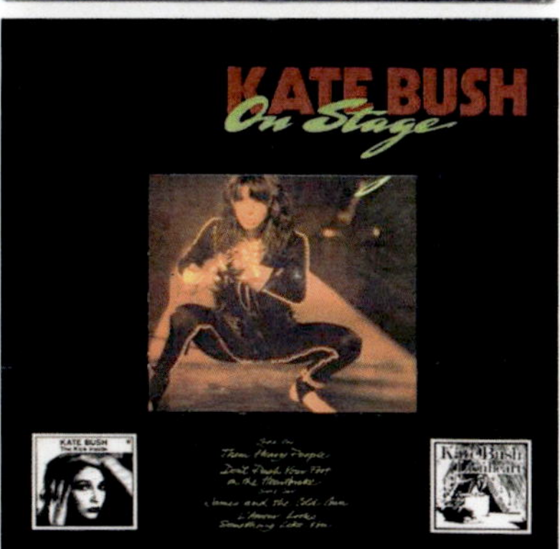

Can.

B & H Records using the DPM system or Direct Plastic Mastering.

000001 The Saxophone Song
000002 Moving
000003 Strange Phenomena
000747 All We Ever Look For
000748 All The Love
000749 Babooshka
000750 Blow Away (For Bill)
000751 Breathing
000752 Coffee Homeground
000753 Delius (Song Of Summer)
000754 Don't Push Your Foot
000755 Egypt
000756 Feel It
000757 Fullhouse
000758 Get Out Of My House
000759 Hammer Horror
000760 Houdini
000761 In Search Of Peter Pan
000762 In The Warm Room
000763 James & The Cold Gun
000764 Kashka From Baghdad
000765 Kite
000766 L'Amour Looks Something
000767 Leave It Open
000768 Night Of The Swallow
000769 Night Scented Stock / Army

000770 Oh England My Lionheart
000771 Oh To Be In Love
000772 Pull Out The Pin
000773 Room For The Life
000774 Sat In Your Lap
000775 Suspended In Gaffa
000776 Symphony In Blue
000777 The Dreaming
000778 The Infant Kiss
000779 The Kick Inside
000780 The Man With The Child
000781 Them Heavy People
000782 There Goes A Tenner
000783 The Wedding List
000784 Violin
000785 Wow
000786 Wuthering Heights
000863 Be Kind To My Mistakes
000865 Don't Give Up (with Gabriel)
Stambul XL 2521 - Hounds Of Love

The next sets are made by Polpress in packages of six. Only 10 sets made by Polpress each set in a white wrap around wallet. Hounds Of Love 6 cards Polpress DR 107, Never Forever 6 cards Polpress DR 108
The Sensual World, This Woman's Work, Reaching Out, Saxophone Song, Strange Phenomena, Moving

The Single File
EMI KBS 1 (UK) Box set with the first 11 British singles plus Ne T'Enfuis Pas/ Un Baiser D'Enfant . Originally numbered and then re issued unnumbered. This contained the only British pressing of "Ne T'Enfuis Pas/ Un Baiser D'Enfant".

Rocket Man – Candle In The Wind
Mercury TRIBO 2 (UK) with poster sleeve and picture sleeve

The Man I Love/Rhapsody In Blue
Mercury MER 408

King Of The Mountain/Sexual Healing
EMI EM674 (UK) Pic Disc

UK

UK

UK

UK

CASSETTE SINGLES

Experiment IV - Wuthering Heights (New Vocal) - December Will Be Magic
TCGOOD 155 (New Zealand)

The Sensual World - Walk Straight Down The Middle
EMI TCEM 102 - (UK)
EMI 2295 (Australia)

This Woman's Work - Be Kind To My Mistakes
EMI TCEM 119 (UK)
EMI 2341 (Australia)

Love And Anger - Be Kind To My Mistakes
EMI TCEM 134 (UK)
EMI Capitol 4JM 73108 (Canada) with different sleeve to UK version.
EMI Capitol 9870 73092 4 (US)
EMI2384 (Australia)

Can.

UK

USA

UK

UK

NZ

12 INCH SINGLES

Running Up That Hill(Remix) / Running Up That Hill Instr. - Under The Ivy
EMI (UK) 12KB1
EMI America V7865 1/2 (US) 33RPM
EMI Capitol V 75115 (Canada)
EMI 1564596 (France)
EMI ED 125 (Australia)

USA

Fra.

Running Up That Hill / Under The Ivy - Running Up That Hill Instr.
EMI 052 200758 (Spain) side 2 tracks reversed to UK version,45RPM.

Cloudbusting (The Organon Mix) / Burning Bridge - My Lagan Love
EMI 12KB2 (UK)
EMI Germany
EMI ED 151 (Australia)
EMI S14-129 (Japan)

Alternative Hounds Of Love / The Handsome Cabin Boy - Jig Of Life
EMI 12KB3 - (UK)

The Big Sky (Meteorological Mix)/ Not This Time - The Morning Fog
EMI 12KB4 (UK)
EMI America S75144 (US and Canada)
EMI ED 212 (Australia)

Spa.

UK

Japan

UK

UK

Experiment IV (12" mix) / Wuthering Heights (New Vocal) - December Will Be Magic Again
EMI 12KB5 (UK)
EMI K060 (Europe)
EMI PM 212 (France)
EMI ED239 (Australia)

The Sensual World / The Sensual World Instr. - Walk Straight Down the Middle
EMI 12EM 102 (UK) Also available with poster cover.
EMI 060 2034946 (Germany)

This Woman's Work / Be Kind To My Mistakes - I'm Still Waiting
EMI 12EM 119 (UK) Also available with a limited edition poster sleeve 12EMP 119.
EMI 060 2036126 (Germany)

Love And Anger / Ken - The Confrontation - One Last Look Around The House Before We Go..
EMI 12EM 134 (UK)
EMI 060 2037536 (Germany)

Rocket Man – Candle In The Wind – Candle In The Wind (Instrumental)
Mercury TRIB 212 (UK)

UK

UK

UK

UK

UK

UK

Rubberband Girl – Rubberband Girl Extended Mix – Big Stripey Lie
EMI 12EMPD280 (UK) Picture disc Also released in an unofficial package with a Baktobak Interview disc BUSHBAK 220066.

UK

Moments of Pleasure – Moments of Pleasure Instrumental – Home For Christmas
EMI 12EMP297 (UK) in Poster sleeve

PROMOS

The Kick Inside Promo Items

USA

Kate Bush Self Portrait The Kick Inside
EMI SSA 3020 US promo album with music and interviews.

The Kick Inside White Label test pressing with photos and biography, (UK).

The Kick Inside test pressing with photos and insert, (Japan).

The Kick Inside test pressing with photos and insert, (Germany).

Them Heavy People/ The Man With The Child In His Eyes
EMR-20490 (Japan w/sticker)

Moving/ Wuthering Heights
PRP 1046

Japan

Japan

Japan

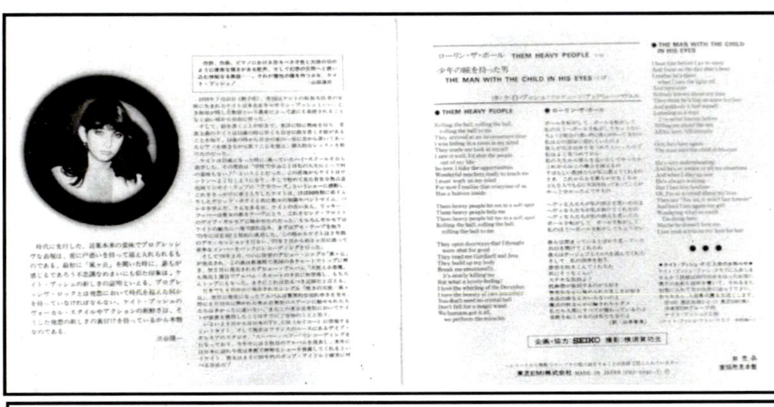

Japan

Japan

Japan

Them Heavy People/ The Man With The Child In His Eyes

PRP 1047 Seiko promotional double 7" single set in deluxe gatefold cover. Two different covers one featuring Kate inside and one featuring the lyrics. Extremely rare,the cover with the picture of Kate inside was limited to 25 copies the second pressing was 200 copies. Probably the rarest Kate Bush record set. Picture left and above.

Japan

Ita.

On Stage

Double single set in gatefold cover.

Them Heavy People/Don't Push Your Foot On The Heartbrake

EMI PSR 442 UK promo

James & The Cold Gun/ L'Amour Looks Something Like You

EMI PSR 443 UK Promo

Wuthering Heights/ Bella La Botega Dell' Arte

3C 000 79019 (Italy) Jukebox promo with other artist on side B.

USA

Wuthering Heights

Sample copy with picture sleeve and round KT logo

Wuthering Heights / Wuthering Heights

PRO 8841 (US) promo with picture sleeve. Mono/ Stereo

Wuthering Heights / Wuthering Heights

8841/ 4589 (Canada) promo 7" M and St

Can.

UK

Can.

USA

Man With The Child In His Eyes/ Moving
Harvest P 1 72798 (Canada) promo 7”

Them Heavy People/Them Heavy People
US promo 12” (Mono)

Reader’s Digest The Sensational 70’s
RD SEN 923 (UK) 5” promo flexi disc Featuring extract from Man With The Child In His Eyes

A Harvest Sampler
US promo sampler features one KB track ‘Man With the Child In His Eyes’ SPRO 8795/SPRO 8796

USA

Debut LP
Debut 8942 German compilation featuring an interview with Kate.

Ger.

10th Anniversary of EMI Records Production And Distribution
EMI (UK) The cover and label do not list who is on this album which was given away as a souvenir disc to visitors to the EMI Hayes Middlesex facility on June 20th 1982, features ‘Wuthering Heights’.

Lionheart promo items

Hammer Horror/ Marras
3C 000 79052 (Italy) Jukebox promo with other artist on B side.

Ita.

Symphony in Blue
Harvest P1-72807 (Canada) Mono

Can.

Lionheart
(Canada) promo music & interview cassette with black and white cover. No serial number, features all of the music from the album with comments by Kate between the songs.

Can.

Never For Ever promo items

Never For Ever
UK promo 3 track flexi disc including excerpts from Egypt, Blow Away, & Delius SFI 562

BBC Transcription Disc Top Of The Pops 821 147081 (UK) Featuring Babooshka

Babooshka/ Damello (Bianca Berg)
EMI 3C 000 79152 (Italy) jukebox promo with other artist on B side

December Will Be Magic
UK promo on green vinyl.

Musical Times
EMI Electrola P528009 (Germany) compilation featuring Army Dreamers

The Dreaming promo items

The Dreaming
EMI SPRO 9847/8 (US) promo 12" featuring Suspended In Gaffa, Pull Out The Pin, Sat In Your Lap, There Goes A Tenner

The Dreaming
EMI SPRO 216 (Canada) promo album with deluxe black and white jacket.

S1. The Dreaming, Suspended In Gaffa Leave It Open S2. Wuthering Heights James And The Cold Gun, Hammer Horror, Wow, Babooshka, Breathing

Suspended In Gaffa
(US) 12" promo single

Super Sampler
SPRO 218 (Canada) Promo Sampler album with one KB track 'The Dreaming'

UK

UK

Ger.

USA

Can.

Japan

Can.

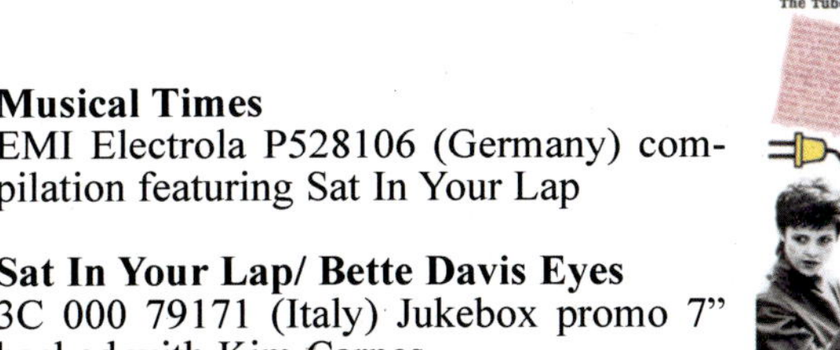

Ger.

Musical Times
EMI Electrola P528106 (Germany) compilation featuring Sat In Your Lap

Sat In Your Lap/ Bette Davis Eyes
3C 000 79171 (Italy) Jukebox promo 7" backed with Kim Carnes

The Abbey Road Collection
EMI PSLP 366 (UK) 50th anniversary album for EMI featuring Sat In Your Lap

Lady's Vocal '83
EMI PRP-8221 (Japan) All The Love

Hounds Of Love promo items

An Interview With Kate Bush
SPRO 282 (Canada) promo album came in ribboned cover

Hounds Of Love
US white label promo with photos and biography, tied in ribbon

Hounds Of Love
12" test pressing (one sided) (UK)

Hounds Of Love
SPRO 9575 (US) promo 12" with long and short versions

Hound Of Love
SPRO 9605 6 (US) long and short versions

Running Up That Hill
Promo 7" in deluxe cover (Spain)

USA

Can.

Ita.

Ita.

USA

Arg.

Ita.

Cloudbusting
US promo 12" with picture sleeve.

Running Up That Hill/ Duran Duran View To A Kill
DIF 362A B (Argentina) promo 7"

Hounds Of Love interview
KBP 1 (Italy) 7" disc promo only with insert picture card.

Running Up That Hill (Extended Version)/ Running Up That Hill
SPRO 9464/9465 (US) promo 12" with deluxe cover.

Running Up That Hill/ Belle Luis Some
1793007 (Italy) Jukebox promo 7" with different artist on B side.

Wholly Virgin NEW TESTAMENTS
Virgin SCROLL 12 (Canada) Compilation cassette made to look like a bible. A very unusual piece featuring Running Up That Hill but from Virgin records.

The Big Sky(Single mix) / The Big Sky
SPRO 9701 (US) promo 12" with picture sleeve

The Big Sky
12KB4 (UK) 12" promo

Rock Over London
Radio Broadcast album RL 248 Interview

Japan

Kate Bush Message
SAMPLE E 7228 Japanese Fan club red flexi disc with interview and live recording of "Let it Be". Possibly a bootleg.

1984 On The Dance Floor & More
EMI SPRO 9077/78 (US) includes "Wow"

Cloudbusting
Cloudbusting - The Man With The Child In His Eyes - Sat In Your Lap - Cloudbusting (Meteorological Mix)
EMI America DPRO 79002 (US) promo CD with four colour deluxe cover.

USA

USA

USA

USA

Japan

Japan

Can.

Japan

UK

Whole Story promo items

Experiment IV EMI SPRO 9892 (US) 12”

Experiment IV
KB5 A (UK) White label test pressing in display box

Experiment IV/ Experiment IV
PB 8363 (US) promo 7” with deluxe cover

Experiment IV
EMI 17676 (Japan) Promo 7” w pic sleeve

The Sensual World promo items

The Sensual World/ Walk Straight Down The Middle PRP 1423 (Japan) promo white label 7” with unique deluxe cover only 50 copies made.

The Sensual World (UK) 3 track promo 12” with double groove on A side.

The Sensual World/ The Sensual World - Walk Straight Down the Middle
12 EM 102 A B (UK) Promo 12”

The Sensual World An Interview With Roger Scott EMI SPRO 458 (Canada) promo cassette with deluxe sleeve.

Can.

The Sensual World - Walk Straight Down The Middle
EMI Capitol 4JM 73098 (Canada)
The Sensual World promo press kit Includes Canadian picture disc CD, cassette single of The Sensual World, 8 page colour booklet with pictures, 2 page bio booklet, all in a plastic case with a deluxe cover. Accompanied by a 12" X 9" folder which contains a synopsis of the Canadian marketing strategy, the lyrics to Sensual World, an Artist profile sheet and an 8 x 10 black and white glossy of Kate.

Can.

Earth News
Westwood One Radio show with Kate interview (US) #90-11

Be Kind To Mistakes/ Chemistry (ENO)
7P518705 (German) promo 7"

USA

WESTWOOD ONE RADIO NETWORKS

Earth News
Show #90-11 for broadcast the week of March 12, 1990

Show 6 - 2:45 Side 2	Incue:	"In his book..."
	Content:	Wes Smith, author of "The Pied Piper Of Rock 'N Roll", explores radio's famous payola scandals of the 60's.
	Commercial:	:30 Halls / :30 Trident
	Outcue:	"...tastes great too."
Show 7 - 2:32 Side 2	Incue:	"No matter how..."
	Content:	Singer Allanah Miles explains why she refuses to succumb to sexist stereotypes.
	Commercial:	:30 Halls / :30 Trident
	Outcue:	"...tastes great too."
Show 8 - 2:28 Side 2	Incue:	"Allanah Myles has..."
	Content:	Singer Allanah Myles recalls the not-so-smooth making of the video to her single, "Black Velvet."
	Commercial:	:30 Halls / :30 Trident
	Outcue:	"...tastes great too."
Show 9 - 2:44 Side 2	Incue:	"The Sensual World..."
	Content:	Singer Kate Bush discusses her work with the popular Trio Bulgarka on her new album, "The Sensual World."
	Commercial:	:30 Halls / :30 Trident
	Outcue:	"...tastes great too."
Show 10 - 2:32 Side 2	Incue:	"Kate Bush isn't..."
	Content:	Singer/songwriter Kate Bush tells why she welcomes each and every interpretation and misinterpretation her music draws.
	Commercial:	:30 Halls / :30 Trident
	Outcue:	"...tastes great too."

Love And Anger
Columbia CSK 1859 (US) promo 5" picture disc with four color deluxe gatefold cover.

This Woman's Work
Columbia CSK 2029 (US) promo 5" with deluxe four colour sleeve.

Sensual World
EMI SPRO - (Canada) Promo 5" 200 imported from the UK

USA

Ger.

Japan

The Sensual World Promotional Sampler
TOSHIBA EMI - SPCD-1082 (Japan)
Only 300 made. Cardboard sleeve

Japan

The Sensual World – Walk Straight Down the Middle
EMI TODP-2110 (Japan)

The Red Shoes Promo Items

UK

Rubberband Girl
EMI GIRL1 (UK) (spoken message, 400 copies, red promo cover)

Rubberband Girl
SPCD-1680 (France) Cardboard sleeve

UK

Rubberband Girl
EMI CDEMDJ280 (UK) (500 copies, black promo cover)

Fra.

UK

Eat the Music – And So Is Love – Top Of The City
EMI CDEMDDJ1047 (UK) 500 made

Tracks From The Red Shoes
EMI (UK) Four track sampler

Moments Of Pleasure
EMI CDEMDJ297 (UK) only 400 made

Rubberband Girl (edit) – Rubberband Girl
Columbia CSK5504 (USA)

The Red Shoes shoebox
Includes album, video of Rubberband Girl and Moments of Pleasure from TV show "Aspel & Co." biography, 35mm slide, and pen. Limited to 1000 copies (UK)

The Red Shoes
EMI CDEMDJ316 (UK) Only 400 made

And So is Love
EMI- DPRO 855 (Canada)

And So Is Love
EMI CDEMDJ355 (UK) Only 400 made

Eat The Music
EMI SPCD-1716 (France) w/ pic sleeve

Moments of Pleasure
Double sampler CD
Toshiba-EMI SPCD-1402/3 (Japan) Inc.

UK

UK

UK

Can.

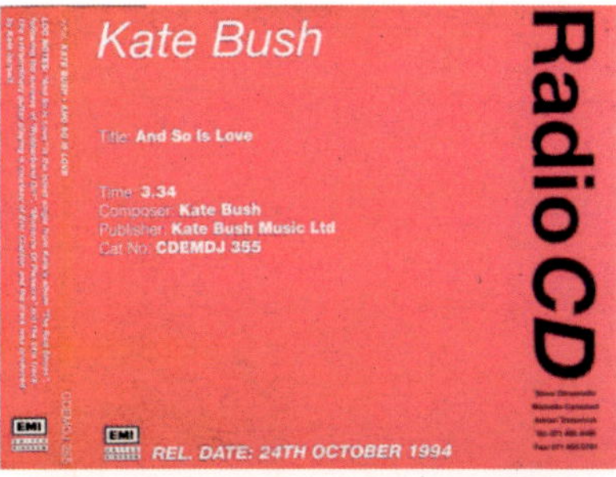

Fra.

UK

Rubberband Girl, And So Is Love, .Eat The Music, Moments Of Pleasure, The Red Shoes, Why Should I Love You, You're The One, Rubberband Girl,.Eat The Music,Moving, The Saxophone Song, The Man With The Child In His Eyes, Wuthering Heights, Symphony In Blue, Wow, Babooshka, The Wedding List, Violin, Army Dreamers, Sat In Your Lap, The Dreaming, Running Up That Hill, Hounds Of Love, The Big Sky, Cloudbusting, The Sensual World, his Woman's Work, December Will Be Magic Again, Un Baiser D'Enfant, Experiment IV, Running Up That Hill, Cloudbusting

Japan

USA

Aerial promo items

King Of The Mountain
EMI CDEMDJ674 CD Pic discw/lyrics

Miscellaneous promo items

Don't Give Up / Don't Give Up
Geffen 28463 (US)

Don't Give Up/ In Your Eyes
(Special Mix)
Virgin PGSDJ 2 (UK)

Don't Give Up (Edit)/ Don't Give Up
Geffen PRO A2689 12" US promo with deluxe cover.

Can

Don't Give Up/ In Too Deep
Virgin JBV 284 (Italy) Jukebox promo 7" with Genesis on side B.

Don't Give Up/ Curtains
Geffen 92 846 37 (Canada) 7" w pic sleeve

Kate Bush
BBC 1980 radio show LP

Kate Bush & Peter Gabriel
BBC 1986 radio show LP

Eur.

USA

Secret Policeman's Third Ball
490643 (US) Promo cassette

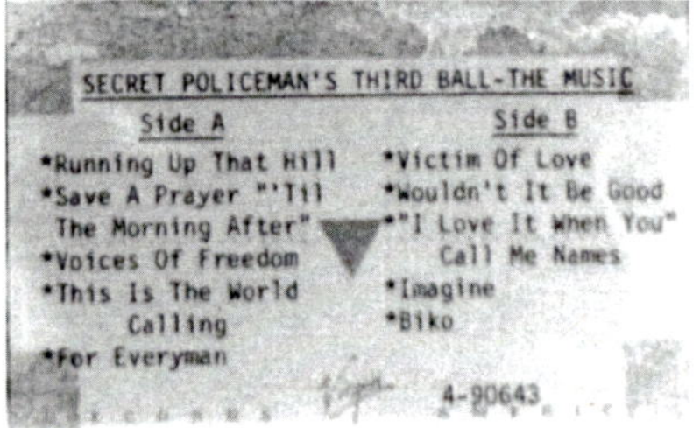

The Glory Of Gershwin
(UK Promo tape in long box)

Christmas 1989
CD PRO Vol #2 (Canada) with December Will Be Magic

Don't Give Up (Edit) - Don't Give Up
(LP Version)
Geffen PRO CD 2680 (US) Peter Gabriel promo 5" deluxe colour gatefold cover.

Interview discs

KB7 (UK) two versions of same interview one on white vinyl one on colour pic disc.

Chat With The Stars Interview ZUFG 006

PROMO 1PD 12 Abbey road interview 12" picture disc

BUSH 7S Die cut picture interview disc, also available as regular 12" with same picture, and as a 7"

BUSH 7 Interview (UK) white vinyl interview 7"

KB1011 12" (UK) Interview Picture disc

CLOUDBUS10 DISCUSSION Gold vinyl

BAK 2006 (UK) Colour 12" picture disc
KB1011 (UK) Interview 12" picture disc

KATE BUSH 7" Interview (UK) five different colours Black, Blue, Red, Yellow, Green with KT logo on the labels.

Interview CD's

Conversation Discs Series
ABCD 012 Colour picture disc Limited edition of 2500 copies. Also available in a 12" deluxe colour box.(UK)

Greyhound KB 7CD 1986 Interview disc in picture sleeve. The interview on this disc is also a part of the interview featured on the Conversation Disc series ABCD 012. 7" quantities pressed on the following vinyl: Black 2,000, Green 500 , Yellow 500 , Red 500 , Blue 500, White 1,000 , Clear 100 , picture disc 2,000. 3" CD 1,000, 5" gold CD 500.

Abbey Road Interview PROMO 1 Numbered limited edition colour sleeve 5" CD

Baktobak Interview CD limited edition with interviews from 1982 and 1985 CBAK 4011

Interview Box Set
BUSH 7 CD (UK) interviews from 1985 and 1986 with two pictures a numbered box and a picture disc CD, extended version of die cut picture disc BUSH 7S.

PROMO 1 (UK/France)
Carboard sleeve only 1000 copies

BUSH 7CD (UK)
Interview for the Dreaming and Hounds of Love comes in box with two pics.

Baktabak / CBAK 4011 (UK) Interview for Dreaming & Hounds of Love

Discussion Records - NEVER 4 CD (UK) Interview Comes in box with three pics

WORDS ABOUT MUSIC
KATE BUSH
Limited Edition Interview Disc

THE CONVERSATION DISC SERIES
KATE BUSH

LIMITED·EDITION
KATE BUSH
Interview Picture Disc
CBAK 4011
INTERVIEW 1: 1982 - THE DREAMING
INTERVIEW 2: 1985 - HOUNDS OF LOVE
COMPACT disc DIGITAL AUDIO
LIMITED EDITION PICTURE DISC INTERVIEW
KATE BUSH

Kate Bush
on compact disc
C.I.D.
LIMITED EDITION BOX SET

KATE BUSH
INTERVIEW

KATE BUSH

BOOTLEG VINYL*

#1 Babooshka Demo & Message
Source: Studio Date: - Cover: D2C Labels: plain white Recording: GS Company: Geil Matrix #: - Country Of Origin: Japan
N.B. Japanese 7" acetate featuring one studio demo of Babooshka and a message.

#2 Back Sides
Source: Studio Pirate Date: N/A Cover: DBW Labels: Deluxe Recording: EXS Company: Pink Frost Matrix #: MS 1A B Country Of Origin: Europe
N.B. This is a pirate of Kate's B sides. Most of this material was released on the vinyl title "Passing Through Air". All of it was made available in the official box sets.

S1. December Will Be Magic Again - Warm & Soothing - Ran Tan Waltz - Full House - The Empty Bullring
S2. Burning Bridge - Not This Time - The Handsome Cabin Boy - Under The Ivy - The Big Sky

 # 3 A Bird In The Hand
Source: Hammersmith London Date: 5/13/79 Cover: D2C Labels: B & W Recording: EXM Company: Heavy Matrix #: CSR 002 A B Country Of Origin: USA
N.B. The cover doesn't have Kate's name on it. It is printed with red type and blue pictures. Taken from the video but recorded in mono.

S1. Violin - Strange Phenomena Hammer Horror - Wow - Feel It
S2. Kite - Oh England My Lionheart - Wuthering Heights - Moving

#4 Cathy's Album
Source: Home Demos Date: 1973 - Cover: D2C Labels: Deluxe Recording: EXM Company: Matrix #: KHD 1126 A B Country Of Origin: USA
N.B. The famous unreleased demo tapes from the pre Gilmour days. Although the

recording is not perfect it is more than adequate. The unreleased material is a real pleasure to hear, and the early versions of familiar material is a treat.

S1. Kashka From Baghdad - Coming Up - Oh, To Be In Love - Playing Canasta - Snow - Ferry Me Over - Lionhearts - Violin - S2. Craft Of Love - Queen Eddie - In My Garden - Frightened Eyes - Never The Less - Goodnight Baby - So Soft - I Don't See Why I Shouldn't

#5 Cathy's Album Too
Source: Home Demos Date: 1973 - Cover: D2C Labels: Deluxe Recording: EXM Company: Matrix #: KHD 1127 A B Country Of Origin: USA N.B. The second volume in the set. More of this piece is familiar material. The same quality as volume one.

S1. The Kick Inside - Hammer Horror - A Rose Growing Old - Keep Me Waiting - Davy - Disbelieving Angel
S2. Don't Push Your Foot On The Heartbrake - Kite - L'Amour Looks Something Like You - Strange Phenomena - Moving - Really Gets Me Going

#6 Dreamtime
Source: London Palladium Date:April 1979 Cover: D4C Labels: Pharting Pharoah Recording: GM Company: Pharting Pharoah Matrix #: 13155 A F Country Of Origin: USA N.B. The controversial cover on this piece caused quite a storm in the fanzines. The naked pictures on the back cover came from a Penthouse spread of a British girl called Kate Simmons who according to Penthouse was a poet, singer, songwriter. Although the pictures used do not bear much resemblance to Kate Bush, some of the dressed shots of Kate Simmons in the article are uncanny in their similarity. Take my word for it, these pictures are not Kate Bush. The recording is mediocre, it's a pity that such an otherwise nice packaging job had to be rendered so tastelessly.

S1. Moving - Saxophone Song - Room For The Life - Them Heavy People - Man With The Child In His Eyes
S2. Egypt - L'Amour Looks Something Like You - Violin - The Kick Inside - The Warm Room
S3. Fullhouse - Strange Phenomena - Hammer Horror - Kashka From Baghdad
S4. Don't Push Your Foot On The Heartbrake - Wow - Coffee Homeground - In Search Of Peter Pan
S5. Symphony In Blue - Feel It - Kite
S6. James And The Cold Gun - Oh England My Lionheart - Wuthering Heights

*Bootleg records are manufactured illegally and, as such, no money goes to the artist. Quality can be extremely poor.

#7 If You Could See Me Fly

Source: Studio** - London Palladium* - Hammersmith Odeon Date: * 28/3/87 - 12/5/79 Cover: D3C Labels: Plain white Recording: GS Company: - Matrix #: KB 200A B Country Of Origin: Europe N.B. This is not the same material as the CD of the same name. Most of it is from the Bill Duffield concert, with the focus on Peter Gabriel's and Steve Harley's songs. Kate is featured extensively on back up vocals and keyboards.

S1. Let It Be * - The Girl With The Child In Her Eyes - Here Comes The Flood - I Don't Remember S2. DIY - The Best Years Of Our Lives - Make Me Smile - Let It Be Babooshka ** - Babooshka 2 **

#8 Kate Bush Fan Club EP

Source: Pirate of Japanese fan club EP Date: Cover: DBW Labels: Deluxe Company: Matrix#: KB PRO 001 1 Country Of Origin: USA N.B. This is a pirate of the original Japanese fan club flexi disc. There is no company name or labels.

S1. Kate Bush Message S2. Let It Be

#9 Kathy Demos Vols 1 5

Source: Studio Date: - Cover: DBW Labels: Deluxe Recording: EXM Company: Matrix#: KB 001 005 Country of Origin: USA N.B. Set of five 7" singles on coloured vinyl.

Volume One
S1. The Kick Inside - Hammer Horror
S2. Rose Growing Old - Keeping Me Waiting

Volume Two
S1. Kashka From Baghdad - Camilla - Oh To Be In Love
S2. In My Lovers Room - Snow Bowl

Volume Three
S1. Ferry Me Over - On The Rocks - Violin
S2. Craft Of Love - Eddie - Garden By The Willow

Volume Four
S1. Frightened Eyes - Disbelieving Angel - Never The Less
S2. Goodnight Baby - To Be With You

Volume Five
S1. Fly Away - Davy
S2. Organic Acid

#10 Live In Bristol England 1979
Source: Bristol Date: 4/9/79 Cover: D4C gatefold Labels: Rock Solid Recording: GM Company: Rock Solid Matrix #: KB 3A B 4A B Country Of Origin: USA
N.B. This really has one of the nicest covers ever seen on a bootleg. It is a gatefold that opens in the centre of the front to reveal another flap inside which has mirror image pictures of Kate Unfortunately the recording quality is barely listenable.

S1. Moving - Saxophone Song - Room For The Life - Them Heavy People - Man With The Child In His Eyes - Egypt - L'Amour Looks Something Like You

S2. Violin - The Kick Inside - In The Warm Room - Fullhouse - Strange Phenomena - Hammer Horror

S3. Kashka From Baghdad - Don't Push Your Foot On The Heartbrake - Wow - Coffee Homeground - In Search Of Peter Pan - Symphony In Blue

S4. Feel It - Kite - James And The Cold Gun - Oh England My Lionheart - Wuthering Heights

#11 Live In Europe 79 & 80
Source: Re issue of "Wow" Date:5/13/79 12/28/79 Cover: Slk Labels: Full Disclosure Recording: EXS and VGM Company: International Matrix #: RSR 203 A D Country Of Origin: USA N.B. This is taken from the original plates for "Wow".

#12 Live In Europe 79 & 80
Source: Re issue of "Wow" and "Paris France 1979" Date:5/13/79 12/28/79 5/6/79 Cover: D4C Labels: Continuing Saga Recording: EXS and VGM Company: International Matrix #: RSR 203 A D, RSR 106A B Country Of Origin: USA N.B. Another re issue of the Rock Solid title, combined with another International title. The first Kate Bush bootleg to appear with a full colour cover.

#13 Live In Japan
Source: Tokyo Budokan* / TVSG Studio Date:18/6/78* 23/6/78 Cover: D4C Labels: Deluxe Recording: VGM Company: IVY GIRL Matrix#: IVY 1A B Country Of Origin: USA
N.B. Very nicely packaged 7" single.

S1. Moving *
S2. She's Leaving Home - The Long & Winding Road

#14 Live In Manchester April 10th 1979
Source: Manchester Date: 4/10/79 Cover: D4C Labels: Rock Solid Recording: GS Company: Rock Solid Matrix #: 10479 A D Country Of Origin: USA N.B. Another nice colour jacket, this one from Rock Solid. Not a very good recording of another 79 concert.

S1. Moving - Saxophone Song - Room For The Life - Them Heavy People - The Man With The Child In His Eyes - Egypt
S2. L'Amour Looks Something Like You - Violin - The Kick Inside - In The Warm Room - Fullhouse

S3. Strange Phenomena - Kashka From Baghdad - Wow - Coffee Homeground - In Search Of Peter Pan
S4. Symphony In Blue - Feel It - James And The Cold Gun - Oh England My Lionheart

#15 Moving
Source: Re issue of "Wow" Date: 5/13/79 - 12/28/79 Cover: D4C Labels: Keri Recording: EXS and VGM Company: Stereo Master Matrix #: RSR 203 A D RR Country Of Origin: Europe N.B. Another re issue of "Wow" with similar matrix numbers but not from the original plates. A nice deluxe colour cover, also pressed on red vinyl to look more like the US original.

#16 Passing Through Air
Source: Various Studios Date: Various Cover: D4C front B&W back Labels: Rock Solid Recording: EXS Company: Rock Solid Matrix #: KB 1A B 2A B Country Of Origin: USA N.B. This is mostly pirated tracks straight from the official releases. A combination of 'B' sides and alternative mixes from 12" singles. Track one on side three is from the Prince's Trust Video, while the last track on side four is from the benefit concert for Bill Duffield. A nice package if you couldn't find the originals.

S1. Cloudbusting (Video mix) - Hounds Of Love (Live BPI awards show) - Experiment IV (Extended mix) - Handsome Cabin Boy - My Lagan Love
S2. Burning Bridge - Not This Time - Big Sky (Astrological Mix) - Under The Ivy
S3. The Wedding List (Live) - Running Up That Hill (Instrumental) Hounds Of Love (Alternate mix) - The Empty Bullring - Dreamtime
S4. Cloudbusting (The Organon Mix) - Passing Through Air - Lord Of The Reedy River - Warm And Soothing - Let It Be (Live)

#17 Paris France 1979

Source: Paris Date: 5/6/79 Cover: Slk Labels: Rock Solid Recording: VGM Company: International Matrix #: RSR 106 A B Country Of Origin: USA N.B. The second Kate Bush bootleg to appear. A better than average recording of part of the Paris show.

S1. Moving - Saxophone Song - Room For The Life - Them Heavy People - The Man With The Child In His Eyes
S2. Egypt - L'Amour Looks Something Like You - Violin - The Kick Inside - In The Warm Room - Fullhouse

#18 Temple Of Truth

Source: - Date: - Cover: D4C Labels: System Acht Recording: PM Company: Escargino Matrix #: KB1 2 33 835 Country Of Origin: Europe N.B. An unusual cover with no track listings. An excellent quality pressing but an incredibly bad recording. Features the uptempo version of 'Egypt'. It is very difficult to determine which show this is from.

S1. Moving - Room For The Life - Them Heavy People - The Man With The Child In His Eyes - Egypt S2. L'Amour Looks Something Like You - The Kick Inside - Fullhouse - Strange Phenomena

#19 Under The Ivy Bush

Source: Various sources Date: Various Cover: D4C Labels: Deluxe Recording: VGM Company: Cunningham Matrix #: KMD 1125 A B Country Of Origin: Europe N.B. A very nice packaging job. Good quality pressing. A mixture of material from several different sources, tracks one and two from side one and track three from side two are all the studio originals with audience noise. The balance is live except for 'Under The Ivy' which is a demo version from the studio.

S1. Running Up That Hill - Big Sky - James And The Cold Gun - Gymnopedies - Symphony In Blue S2. Man With The Child In His Eyes - Violin - Hammer Horror - Kite - Wuthering Heights - Under The Ivy

#20 What Katie Did For Amnesty International
Source: London Palladium Date: 28/3/87 Cover: D2C Labels:Deluxe Company: Royal Matrix#: DAVY 02A B Country Of Origin: UK N.B. Nicely packaged 7" featuring Kate's performance with Dave Gilmour.

S1. Running Up That Hill
S2. Let It Be

#21 Wow Live
Source: Hammersmith London and Xmas TV special Date: 5/13/79 - 12/28/79 Cover: Slk Labels: Rock Solid Recording: EXS and VGM Company: Rock Solid Matrix #: RSR 203 A D Country Of Origin: USA N.B. This was the first Kate Bush bootleg. 500 numbered copies on red vinyl. A pink and black slick. A good quality pressing, which has been knocked off many times. 2,000 colour picture discs were also made from the original plates. The second disc is from the Christmas special and features Peter Gabriel on two tracks. The first disc is straight from the video.

S1. Moving - Them Heavy People - Violin - Strange Phenomena - Hammer Horror - Don't Push Your Foot On The Heartbrake - Wow
S2. Feel It - Kite - James And The Cold Gun - Oh, England My Lionheart - Wuthering Heights
S3. Violin - Symphony In Blue - Them Heavy People - Here Comes The Flood - Ran Tan Waltz - December Will Be Magic Again
S4. The Wedding List - Another Day - Egypt - The Man With The Child In His Eyes - Don't Push Your Foot On The Heartbrake

CD Bootlegs*

#22 Alone At My Piano
UKINEL 200 (US) The home demo tapes, unfortunately not quite complete. The song titles listed are the titles as they appear on the cover of the tape that circulated. The () are the titles as they appear on this CD.

The Kick Inside, Hammer Horror, A Rose Growing Old (It Hurts Me), Keeping Me Waiting, Kashka From Baghdad, Surrender Into The Roses (Coming Up) , Oh To Be In Love, Geoffrey The Gardener (Playing Canasta), Hot In The Ice (Snow), The Music Dies (Ferry Me Over), (Lionhearts) On The Rocks, Violin, The Craft Of Love, Gay Farewell (Queen Eddie), Something Like A Song (In My Garden), Frightened Eyes, Disbelieving Angel, (Never The Less) You'll Do, Goodnight Baby, I Need You Like Dough (So Soft), Pick The Rare Flowers (I Don't See Why I Shouldn't), Davy Davy (Hold Me)

#23 Back Sides
Observation Records OB 002. This is the same material as the vinyl version. Mostly pirated from the real records complete with crackles.

December Will Be Magic, Warm & Soothing, Ran Tan Waltz, Full House, The Empty Bullring, Burning Bridge, Not This Time, The Handsome Cabin Boy, Under The Ivy, The Big Sky

*Bootleg CDs are manufactured illegally and, as such, no money goes to the artist. Quality can be extremely poor.

#24 Burning Desire
Swingin' Pigs B016 1 (Europe) This is good quality for a bootleg but when you consider the quality of the source material it is unbelievably bad.Taken from the Hammersmith video. Poor packaging, if you can find the Neutral Zone CD of this material it is infinitely preferable, of course the official Laserdisc or CD is even more preferable.

Moving, Them Heavy People, Violin, Strange Phenomena, Hammer Horror, Don't Push Your Foot On The Heartbrake, Wow, Feel It, Kite, James And The Cold Gun, Oh England My Lionheart, Wuthering Heights

#25 If You Could See Me Fly
Chapter One CO 25119 (Europe)
Featuring some early demo material which the cover claims was recorded in 1974. Some clicks and pops but otherwise quite nice. Good packaging with a full color open out cover.The song titles listed are the titles as they appear on the cover of the tape that circulated. The () are the titles as they appear on this CD.

Babooshka, Kashka From Baghdad, Surrender Into The Roses (Coming Up) , Oh To Be In Love, Geoffrey The Gardener (Playing Canasta), Hot In The Ice (Snow), The Music Dies (Ferry Me Over), (Lionhearts) On The Rocks, Violin, The Craft Of Love, Gay Farewell (Queen Eddie), Something Like A Song (In My Garden), Frightened Eyes, (Never The Less) You'll Do, Goodnight Baby, I Need You Like Dough (So Soft), Pick The Rare Flowers (I Don't See Why I Shouldn't), Babooshka Version 2

#26 Live At Hammersmith 1979
Neutral Zone NZCD 89010 (US) The video soundtrack plus two live tracks and one studio pirate track. Very nice full colour packaging. Excellent quality. The first bootleg Kate CD.

Moving, Them Heavy People, Violin, Strange Phenomena, Hammer Horror, Don't Push Your Foot On The Heartbrake, Wow, Feel It, Kite, James And The Cold Gun, Oh England My Lionheart, Wuthering Heights, Running Up That Hill* , Breathing**, This Woman's Work***
* From The Secret Policeman's Third Ball.
** From Utterly Utterly
Live. *** From She's Having A Baby Soundtrack (Different mix to The Sensual World).

#27 Live and Fruity
Orbit Records Compilation of TV and live appearances
1984 Convention Message (spoken by Kate), What If? (Fruitopia), Cloudbusting (Techno Diva Mix), Breathing (live), Comfortably Numb (live with David Gilmour), Fighting Fruit (Fruitopia), Do Bears? (live with Rowan Atkinson) Tokyo Festival Press Release (spoken), The Long and Winding Road (live), She's Leaving Home (live), Raspberry Psychic (Fruitopia) Do Bears? (diff version)Candle in the Wind (Techno Diva Mix)Strawberry Passion (Fruitopia), Dreamtime (Instrumental), Let it Be (live with Peter Gabriel), Teaser (Fruitopia), The Handsome Cabin Boy (non-Kate track)Message of Love (Fruitopia)

#28 Live and Fruity 2
Orbit Records Compilation of TV and live appearances
Fruitopian Ad, Room For The Life (Live Germany 1979) Wuthering Heights (Live Germany 1979), Euphoria (Fruitopia), December Will Be Magic Again (Live 1980), Don't Push Your Foot On The HeartBreak (Live 1980), Them Heavy People (Live 1980), Vision (Fruitopia), Running Up That Hill (Monster Party Mix), Waking The Witch (Special DJ Mix), Wuthering Heights (Hip-Hop Mix), Summer Solstice (Fruitopia), L'Amour Looks Something Like You (Live 1979), The Wedding List (Live 1982), Consciousness (Fruitopia), Running Up That Hill (Live 1987), Mna Na Heireann (Rare Studio Track in Gaelic), Inner Light (Fruitopia)

#29 Passing Through Air
Chapter One CO 25129.
Don't be fooled by the artwork on this one. It is not the same material as the vinyl of the same name. It is mainly the studio rehearsals and home demo stuff again. It is taken from a clear but obviously crackly source. It does feature most of the songs which aren't on "Alone At My Piano". It also includes the performance of Another Day from the Christmas TV Special, and it is the only CD with the demo of "Moving". Very nice deluxe colour open out cover.

The Kick Inside, Hammer Horror, A Rose Growing Old, Keeping Me Waiting, Davy Davy (Hold Me), Disbelieving Angel, Don't Push Your Foot On The Heartbrake, Kite, L'Amour Looks Something Like You Strange Phenomena, Really Gets Me Going, Moving, Another Day

#30 Performed Live In London 1979
Super Golden Radio Shows SGRS 013.
The Hammersmith show without any surprises. Basically inferior to the Neutral Zone version but still very good quality.

Moving, Them Heavy People, Violin, Strange Phenomena, Hammer Horror, Don't Push Your Foot On The Heartbrake, Wow, Feel It, Kite, James And The Cold Gun, Oh England My Lionheart, Wuthering Heights.

#31 Practice Makes Perfect Piano Demos Volume One
91 100 01 (Europe)
Another version of the home demo tapes, this one has most of the tracks but is a bit crackly.The song titles listed are the titles as they appear on the cover of the tape that circulated. The () are the titles as they appear on this CD.

Kashka From Baghdad, Surrender Into The Roses (Coming Up), Oh To Be In Love, Geoffrey The Gardener (Playing Canasta), Hot In The Ice (Snow), The Music Dies (Ferry Me Over), (Lionhearts) On The Rocks, Violin, The Craft Of Love, Gay Farewell (Queen Eddie), Something Like A Song (In My Garden), Frightened Eyes, (Never The Less) You'll Do, I Need You Like Dough (So Soft), Pick The Rare Flowers (I Don't See Why I Shouldn't), The Kick Inside, Hammer Horror, A Rose Growing Old (It Hurts Me), Keeping Me Waiting, Davy Davy (Hold Me), Disbelieving Angel, Don't Push Your Foot On The Heartbrake, Kite, L'Amour Looks Something Like You, Strange Phenomena, Really Gets Me Going

#32 This Woman's Work Live
(Germany) ODY 028 KB 4 A compilation of various performances from TV including Hammersmith

Moments Of Pleasure (U.K. TV 1993), Running Up That Hill (Amnesty Int. 1987) Let It Be (Amnesty Int. 1987), Don't Give Up (London w/Peter Gabriel 1987), Under The Ivy (U.K. TV 1985), The Wedding List (London charity gig 1982, Breathing (U.K. TV 1980), Moving, Violin, Wow, James And The Cold Gun, Oh, England My Lionheart, The Long And Winding Road (Japanese TV 1978), She's Leaving Home (Japanese TV 1978), Wuthering Heights (US TV 78), Man With The Child In His Eyes (US TV 78), Them Heavy People (US TV 78)

#33 Cathy's Home Demos
Blue Moon Records - BMCD-008 (Germany)
Very nice quality of the home demos plus the last five tracks with the KT Bush band.

Babooshka, Kashka From Baghdad, Coming Up, Oh, To Be In Love, Playing Canasta, Snow, Ferry Me Over, Lionhearts, Violin, The Craft Of Love, Queen Eddie, In My Garden, Frightened Eyes, Never The Less, Goodnight Baby, So Soft, I Don't See Why I Shouldn't, Babooshka (Different version), The Kick Inside, Hammer Horror, A Rose Growing Old, Keep Me Waiting, Davy, Disbelieving Angel, Don't Push Your Foot On The Heart Brake, Kite, L'Amour Looks Something Like You, Strange Phenomena

#34 Home Demos
Genuine Pig Records TGP-CD-093 (Italy)

Babooshka, Kashka From Baghdad, Coming Up, Oh, To Be In Love, Playing Canasta, Snow, Ferry Me Over, Lionhearts Violin, The Craft Of Love, Queen Eddie, In My Garden, Frightened Eyes, Never The Less, Goodnight Baby, So Soft, I Don't See Why I Shouldn't, Babooshka (Different version), The Kick Inside, Hammer Horror, A Rose Growing Old, Keep Me Waiting, Davy, Disbelieving Angel, Don't Push Your Foot On The Heart Brake, Kite, L'Amour Looks Something Like You, Strange Phenomena

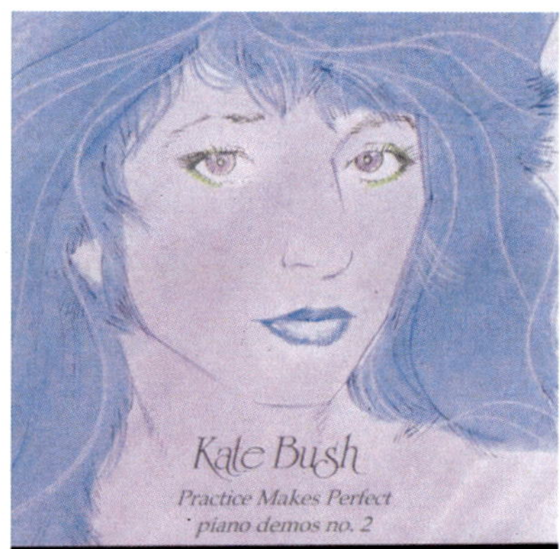

#35 Practice Makes Perfect Piano Demos 2
Barklee (France) Possibly a CD-R only

Atlantis, Come Closer To Me Babe, Sunsi Cussi Cussi, Organic Acid, Maybe, Humming, Moving, Passing Through Air You Were The Star, Babooshka (piano), Babooshka (beat-box), Sat In Your Lap, Radio 1 Yule Jingle, December Will Be Magic, Again (beat-box), The Magician, Sexual Healing, Fruitopia

#36 Shrubberies
Red Robin Records - KBCD 94011 (UK)

The Kick Inside, Hammer Horror, Rose Growing Old, Keep Me Waiting, Kashka From Baghdad, Coming Up, Oh, To Be In Love, Playing Canasta, Snow, Ferry Me Over, Lionhearts, Violin, Craft Of Love, Queen Eddie, In My Garden, Frightened Eyes, Disbelieving Angel, Never The Less Good Night Baby, So Soft, I Don't See Why I Shouldn't, Davy, Babooshka, Moving, Don't Push Your Foot On The Heartbrake, Kite

#37 Kate Bush
VIP 001 (Italy)
Recorded Live In London 1979, another version of Hammersmith

Moving, Them Heavy People, Violin, Strange Phenomena, Hammer Horror, Don't Push Your Foot On The Heartbrake, Wow, Feel It, Kite, James And The Cold Gun, Oh England My Lionheart, Wuthering Heights.

#38 Mystic Lady
ECLIPSE - EML 185 (Australia)
Recorded Live in London and another Hammersmith

Moving, Them Heavy People, Violin, Strange Phenomena, Hammer Horror, Don't Push Your Foot On The Heartbrake, Wow, Feel It, Kite, James And The Cold Gun, Oh England My Lionheart, Wuthering Heights.

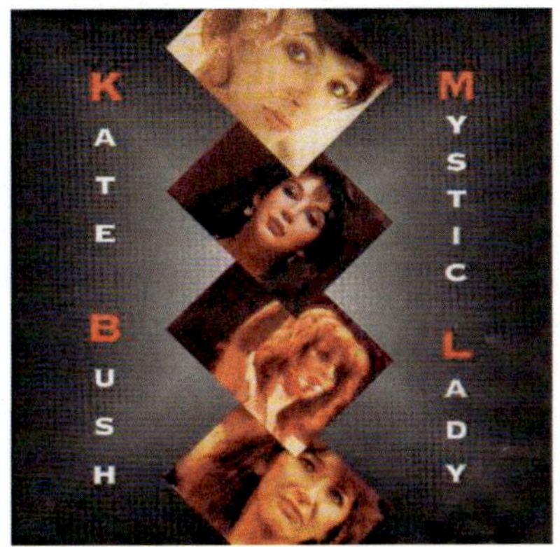

#39 Butterfly Kisses
SCORPIO 007 (Germany) A compilation of rare TV and live appearances

[Top of the Pops, 02/16/78]Wuthering Heights, The Wedding List - [Saturday Night Live 09/12/78] The Man With The Child In His Eyes, Them Heavy People - [Abbey Road March 1986] Under The Ivy - [Comic Relief 04/04/86] Breathing, Do Bears? - [Amnesty International 03/28/87] Running Up That Hill, - [Budokan, Tokyo June 1978] Moving - [Japan 1978] The Long and Winding Road, She's Leaving Home - [Germany May 1979] Room For Life, Strange Phenomena, Violin, In The Warm Room, Kite, Wuthering Heights

#40 Live At The London Palladium
Kojono Records (Europe)

Moving, The Saxophone Song, Room For The Life, Them Heavy People, The Man With The Child In His Eyes, Egypt, L'Amour Looks Something Like You, Violin, The Kick Inside, In The Warm Room, Fullhouse, Strange Phenomena, Hammer Horror, Kashka From Baghdad Don't Push Your Foot On The Heartbrake

Wow, Coffee Homeground, In Search Of Peter Pan, Symphony In Blue, Feel It Kite, James & The Cold Gun, Oh,England My Lionheart, Wuthering Heights

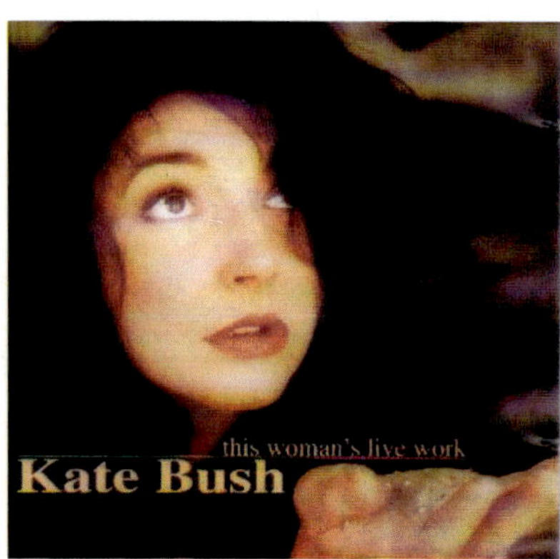

#41 This Woman's Live Work
INVASION UNLIMITED - IU 9304-1 (Germany) Live TV appearances including Saturday Night Live. From Japan, Germany and the UK TV special

Wuthering Heights, Man With The Child In His Eyes, Them Heavy People, Moving The Long And Winding Road, She's Leaving Home, Room For The Life, In The Warm Room, The(Wo)man With The Child, In His(Her) Eyes, Symphomy In Blue, December Will Be Magic Again, Ran Tan Waltz, Egypt, Another Day(w/ Peter Gabriel), Breathing, The Wedding List, Under The Ivy, Running Up That Hill, Don't Give Up(w/Peter Gabriel)
Let It Be

#42 This Woman's Live Work
Crown Of Britain - COB 900 (Europe) Live TV appearances including Saturday Night Live. From Japan, Germany and the UK, Sane track listing as #39 above.

#43 Collaborations
Twilight Music - TMCD 005 (Europe)
Various guest appearances conveniently all accumulated on one disc.

Sing Children Sing (1979 w/Lesley Duncan), Rainbow Games (B-side of the above), Another Day (Live w/Peter Gabriel), The Man With The Child In His Eyes (Live w/Peter Gabriel & Steve Harley), The King Is Dead (From a single w/Go West), Once (Studio track w/Roy Harper), Don't Give Up (Live version w/ Peter Gabriel), Let It Be (Live version w/ Dave Gilmour), Flowers (Duet w/Zane Griff), You(The Game, Part III) (Studio track w/Roy Harper), Do Bears (w/Rowan Atkinson), The Seer (Kate backing Big Country), The Kick Inside, This Woman's Work

#44 Gold Ballads
DOG Entertaiment - DOG 10001 (Europe)
I believe this to be a pirate of studio recordings.

Army Dreamers, Oh, England My Lionheart, Them Heavy People, December Will Be Magic Again, Running Up That Hill, And So Is Love, Ran Tan Waltz, Wuthering Heights, Babooshka, Man With The Child In His Eyes, Under Ice, Egypt, Moving, The Wedding List, Symphony In Blue, Cloudbusting, L'Amour Looks Something Like You, The Sensual World, Don't Push Your Foot On The Heartbrake, Strange Phenomena

#45 Golden Collection
Grave Music Co. - GMC-714 (Europe)
Same as above (#42) Also almost certainly a pirate.

#46 Hit Collection
E.S.RECORDS (Europe)
Pirate of studio material

The Sensual World, Wuthering Heights, Cloudbusting, The Man With The Child In His Eyes, Breathing, Wow, Hounds Of Love, Running Up That Hill ,Don't Give Up, Experiment IV ,The Dreaming, Babooshka, The Fog, .Deeper Understanding, This Woman's Work, And So Is Love, The Red Shoes, You're The One

#47 Kate Bush Complete Collection 1978-1993
(Russia) Pirate MP3 CDROM of the entire catalog up to 1993

#48 Rarities
Five Dollar Records - FDR147 (Europe)
Compilation of odd tracks from various studio sources.

Mna Na Heirann, You Want Alchemy, The Man I Love, Home For Christmas, Show A Little Devotion, Moments Of Pleasure (instrumental version), Don't Give Up, The Sensual World (instrumental version), Cloudbusting (video mix), The Confrontation, Rocket Man ,Candle In The Wind, Dreamtime, Under The Ivy (live), Running Up That Hill (live), Breathing (live), Organic Acid (demo)

#49 This Woman's Work Extended Edition 1
410.353 KB 1 (Europe)
Pirate of B-sides and various rare studio tracks

The Empty Bullring, Ran Tan Waltz, Passing Through Air, December Will Be Magic Again, Warm And Soothing, Lord Of The Reedy River, Ne T'en Fui Pas, Un Baiser D'un Enfant, Under The Ivy, Burning Bridge, My Lagan Love ,The Handsome Cabin Boy, Not This Time, Walk Straight Down The Middle, Be Kind To My Mistakes, Rocket Man, Candle In The Wind

#50 This Woman's Work Extended Edition 2
410.354 KB 2 (Europe)
Pirate of B-sides and various rare studio tracks

I'm Still Waiting, Ken, One Last Look Around The House Before We Go, Wuthering Heights(new vocals), Experiment IV, Them Heavy People, Don't Push Your Foot On The Heartbrake, James & The Cold Gun, L'Amour Looks Something Like You, Running Up That Hill, Cloudbusting (Organon mix), Hounds Of Love(alt. ver.), The Big Sky(met. mix), Experiment IV(12" mix), Rubberband Girl

#51 This Woman's Work Extended Edition 3
ODY 027 KB 3 (Europe)
Pirate of B-sides and various rare studio tracks

Cloudbusting(video mix), Eat The Music(extended mix), You Want Alchemy, Shoedance (the Red Shoe dance mix) , Show A Little Devotion, Moments Of Pleasure (instrumental version), Home For Christmas, Rubberband Girl(extended version), Candle In The Wind (instrumental version), Don't Give Up(w/Peter Gabriel)

VIDEO TAPES

Live At Hammersmith Odeon
TVD 9005032 (UK)
TXD 1952 (US and Canada)
Also released again with a CD of the show (see page 20)

Moving - Them Heavy People - Violin - Strange Phenomena - Hammer Horror - Don't Push Your Foot On The Heartbrake - Wow - Feel It - Kite - James And The Cold Gun - Oh England My Lionheart - Wuthering Heights

The Single File
TVE 9014302 (UK)
TT13 1060FI (Japan with lyric sheet)

Wuthering Heights - The Man With The Child In His Eyes - Hammer Horror - Wow - The Heavy People - Breathing - Babooshka - Army Dreamers - Sat In Your Lap - The Dreaming - Suspended In Gaffa - There Goes A Tenner

The Hair Of The Hound
MVR 9900532 (UK)

Running Up That Hill - Hounds Of Love - The Big Sky - Cloudbusting

The Whole Story
MVP 9911432 (UK)
Sony Video LP RO577 (US and Canada)
JAI VID TT10 1169HI (Japan)

Wuthering Heights - Cloudbusting - The Man With The Child In His Eyes - Breathing - Wow - Hounds Of Love - Running Up That Hill - Army Dreamers - Sat In Your Lap - Experiment IV - The Dreaming - Babooshka - The Big Sky

The Sensual World The Videos
2VS 49034 with interview and three videos (US)

Introduction - Love And Anger - Interlude - The Sensual World - Interlude - This Woman's Work

The Line, the Cross and the Curve
PMI MVN 4911853 (UK)
Columbia 19V-50118 (USA)
Toshiba-EMI TOVW3198 (Japan)

Peter Gabriel Cv
Virgin Music 50118 3 eight videos featuring Kate on two different versions of 'Don't Give Up'

The Big Time - Don't Give Up 2 - Shock The Monkey - Mercy Street - Sledgehammer - I Don't Remember - Red Rain - Don't Give Up 1

Various Artists
The Prince's Trust Rock Gala
MGM/UA MV400179 (US) Includes Kate performing 'Wedding List' with Phil Collins and Pete Townshend.

Bootleg Videos

Kate Bush The Collection
Mirage Video (US) With deluxe four colour case VHS NTSC only.
Includes Wedding List (Prince's Trust) - December Will Be Magic Again(UK TV) - Babooshka (Dr Hook show UKTV) - Delius (UKTV) - Razzmatazz (UKTV Interview) - Wow (British Rock & Pop Awards) - Them Heavy People (UKTV) - Delia Smith's Cookery Show (UKTV) - Russel Hardy Show (UKTV) - Army Dreamers (UKTV) - Desmond Morris Show (UKTV) - The Dreaming (UKTV) - Old Grey Whistle Test - There Goes A Tenner (UKTV Razzmatazz) - Kate Bush Quiz Box (Music Box UKTV)

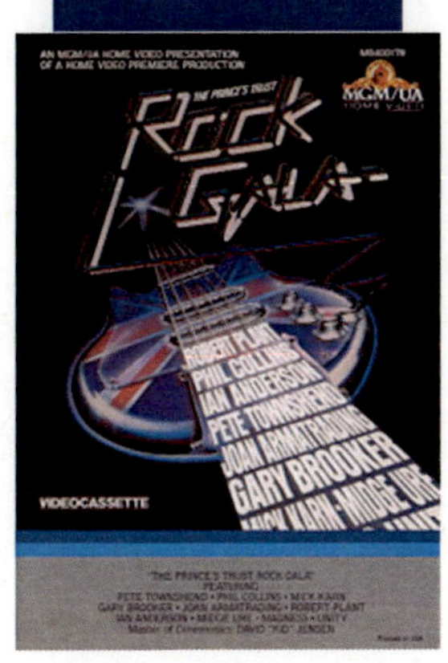

TV appearances

1986 COLLEGE MUSIC AWARDS (USA)
Kate receives an award. 1986. (2 mins).

7TH TOKYO MUSIC FESTIVAL (JAPAN)
"Moving" Live. June 1978. (4 mins).

ABBA SPECIAL (UK)
Mimed performance of "Wow", tape Feb. 1979, aired 21 April 1979. (4 mins).

ASK ASPEL (UK)
Interview and clip of "Wuthering Heights" from Top Of The Pops, and live version of "Kashka From Baghdad". 5 September 1978. (15 mins).

ASPEL & COMPANY (UK)
"Moments of Pleasure" & interview Jun 20 1993

BANANAS (GERMANY)
"Suspended In Gaffa" (puppets version) November 1982. (4 mins).

BIO'S BAHNHOF (GERMANY)
Live performances of "Kite", "Wuthering Heights", Kate's first TV appearance February 1978. (8 mins).

BPI AWARDS (UK)
"Hounds Of Love" live performance. January 10 1986. (5 mins).

BPI AWARDS (UK)
Kate presents and receives awards. An extract of a different version of "Wow". February 1980. (5 mins).

BPI AWARDS (UK)
Kate wins and presents an award. (5 mins).

BRITISH ROCK AND POP AWARDS
2/80 (5 min)

CHAMPS ELYSEES (FRANCE)
"Suspended In Gaffa". (white steps version). October 1982. (4 mins).

CITY PULSE NEWS (CANADA)
Interview and video. 11/85. (2 mins).

CNN (JAPAN)
Interview November 1985. (4 mins).

COLLARD (FRANCE)
"Babooshka" (green dress and cape winter scenery) September 1980. (4 mins).

COLLEGE MUSIC AWARDS
1986 (1 min)

COMIC RELIEF BENEFIT (UK)
"Do Bears... " live with Rowan Atkinson and "Breathing" live. April 1986. (8 mins).

COMIC STRIP (UK)
"G.L.C. - The Carnage Continues". Kate wrote incidental music. February 1990. (35 mins).

COMIC STRIP (UK)
"Les Dogs" Kate's first feature acting role. Filmed January 1990, aired March 1990. (35 mins).

COUNTDOWN (AUSTRALIA)
Interview and "Hammer Horror". 12 October 1978. (12 mins).

COUNTDOWN (HOLLAND)
"Army Dreamers", ("third cigarette" version), October 1980. (4 mins).

COUNTDOWN (HOLLAND)
"Babooshka" (red outfit version). October 1980. (8 mins).

COUNTDOWN (HOLLAND)
Interview. November 1985. (6 mins).

DANCE STUDIO INTERVIEW
8/6/81 (3 min)

DAVE GILMOUR CONCERT (UK)
Performing Comfortably Numb Jan 19 2002

DELIA SMITH COOKERY (UK)
Interview on vegetarian recipes and cooking. February 1980. (6 mins).

DEMAINE C'EST DIMANCHE (FRANCE)
"Running Up That Hill" (Paddy version). September 1985. (5 mins).

DIE EPTELING PARK (HOLLAND)
Video clips filmed in a Gothic Theme park, "Moving", "Wuthering Heights", "Them Heavy People", "The Man With The Child In His Eyes", "Strange Phenomena", "The Kick Inside". April 1978. (20 mins).

DISCO-RING (ITALY)
"The Dreaming" (light show version). September 1982. (5 mins).

DR HOOK (UK)
"Babooshka" (schizoid version, with different audio) "Delius" video clip and interview. Taped March 1980, aired April 1980. (4 mins)

EXTRATOUR (GERMANY)
"Running Up That Hill". (short version). November 1985. (3 mins).

FRIDAY NIGHT SATURDAY MORNING
(UK) Interview. 20 November 1981. (8 mins)

GLOBAL TV (CANADA)
Interview and video clips. 11/85. (4 mins).

GOOD ROCKIN' TONIGHT (CANADA)
Interview and video clips November 1985 (9 mins).

GOOD ROCKIN' TONIGHT (CANADA)
Interview and video clips. November 1985. (6 mins).

HAPPY MAGIC (ITALY)
"The Dreaming" (psychedelic version). Spetember 1982. (5 mins).

HEARTLIGHT CITY
brief interview clip 11/85 1 min

IVOR NOVELLO AWARDS (UK)
May 23 2002 Accepting award

JEU DE LA VERITE (FRANCE)
"Running Up That Hill" September 1985. (5 mins).

KATE - CHRISTMAS SPECIAL (UK)
Live or alternative versions of "Violin", "Symphony In Blue", "Them Heavy People", "Here Comes The Flood", "Ran Tan Waltz", "December Will Be Magic Again", "The Wedding List", "Another Day", "Egypt", "The Man With The Child In His Eyes", "Don't Push Your Foot On The Heartbrake". December 1979. (45 mins).

KATE BUSH IN CONCERT (GERMANY & HOLLAND)
Interview April 1980 & video clips from April and May 1979, including "Room For The Life" and "In The Warm Room" (45 mins).

KENNY EVERETT VIDEO SHOW (UK)
Comedy performance and two videos March 1979 (8 mins).

LEO SAYER SHOW (UK)
"Don't Push Your Foot On The Heartbrake". November 1978. (3 mins).

LET IT BE FERRY AID VIDEO 1987
promo video with one verse by Kate

LIVE AT FIVE (USA)
Interview and video clips. November 1985. (6 mins).

LOOKING GOOD FEELING FIT (UK)
Interview and "Sat In Your Lap" rehearsal. August 1981. (5 mins).

LOVE AND ANGER CBS PROMO Different edit to finished version. October 1989. (5 mins).

MAN I LOVE (THE)
promo video with Larry Adler (4 min)

MTV (USA)
Interview. November 1985. (7 mins).

MTV (USA)
Two interview clips. Nov 1985. (3 mins).

MTV 120 MINUTES (USA)
"X Ray On Kate Bush". Taped December 1989, aired December 1989. Interview and video clips. (5 mins).

MUCH MUSIC (CANADA)
Interview and video clips. November 1985. (12 mins).

MUCH MUSIC (CANADA)
News clip on The Sensual World. October 1989. (1 min).

MUCH MUSIC SPECIAL - THE STORY SO FAR (CANADA)
Interview and video clips Broadcast June 1987, taped April 1987, March and November 1985. (60 mins).

MUCH MUSIC SPOTLIGHT (CANADA)
Interview and video clips with one additional new clip. December 1989. (30 mins).

MUCH MUSIC SPOTLIGHT (CANADA)
Interview and video clips. May 1989. (30 mins).

MULTI COLOURED SWAP SHOP (UK)
Interview and video clips. January 1979. (20 mins).

MUSIC OF THE WORLD (UK)
Interview & studio footage of Trio Bulgarka and Kate. Nov 1988. (6 mins)

MUSICAL CHAIRS (UK)
"Wow" video documentary. March 1979. (7 mins).

NA SOWAS (GERMANY)
"The Dreaming" ("Lizard King" version) September 1982. (5 mins).

NATIONWIDE (UK)
Interview and banned clips from "Breathing" video. (5 mins).

NATIONWIDE (UK)
Kate Bush on Tour Documentary. April 1979. (25 mins).

NEW MUSIC (CANADA)
Interview and video clips. Nov 1985. (7 mins).

NEW MUSIC (CANADA)
Interview and video clips. Taped March 1985, aired November 1985. (8 mins).

NIGHT FLIGHT (USA)
Interview source tape. Nov 1985. (20 mins).

NIGHT FLIGHT VIDEO PROFILE (USA)
Interview and video clips Broadcast March 1986, taped November 1985.(30 mins).

OLD GREY WHISTLE TEST (UK)
Interview and video clips. Sept 1982. (8 mins).

OLD GREY WHISTLE TEST (UK)
Interview. October 1985. (4 mins).

OUR COMMON FUTURE (CANADA)
"Spirit Of The Forest" promo video clip, Kate has one line. June 1989. (4 mins).

PEBBLE MILL AT ONE (UK)
Interview. October 1982. (12 mins).

PETERS POP (GERMANY)
"Running Up That Hill", "The Big Sky", November 1985. (9 mins).

PROFILE 6 (FRANCE)
Interview. September 1985. (25 mins).

PROFILES IN ROCK (CANADA, FILMED IN THE UK)
Interview and video clips December 1980.(30 mins).

Q MAGAZINE AWARDS (UK)
October 29 2001 Accepting award

RAPIDO (UK, FRANCE)
Interview, studio footage. October 1989. (9 mins).

RAZAMATAZZ (UK)
"There Goes A Tenner". 21 September 1982. (4 mins).

RAZAMATAZZ (UK)
Interview and video clips. 14 July 1981. (10 mins).

REVOLVER (UK)
"Them Heavy People". (Live) Taped March 1978, aired May 1978. (4 mins).

RIVA DEL GARDA (ITALY)
"The Dreaming" (stage version). September 1982. (5 mins).

ROCK AROUND THE WORLD (AUSTRALIA)
"Army Dreamers" (beret version) 1980. (4 mins).

ROCKFLIX PROMO FILM
"Wuthering Heights". Feb. 1978. (4 mins).

ROCKLINE (FRANCE)
Interview and video clips. Sept 1985. (7 mins).

ROCKPOP (GERMANY)
Mimed versions of "Babooshka", and "Army Dreamers" (cleaning lady outfit). 2 Sept 1980 (7 mins).

RUSSELL HARTY SHOW (UK)
"Delius" and interview. Nov 1980. (6 mins).

SATURDAY MORNING SHOW (UK)
Interview and "Wuthering Heights" parody. 1979 (7 mins).

SATURDAY NIGHT LIVE (USA)
Live versions of "The Man With The Child In His Eyes", "Them Heavy People". December 1978. (6 mins).

SATURDAY SUPERSTORE (UK)
Interview and video clips. 1 Oct/ 82. (13 mins)

SCENE 78 (GERMANY)
"Wuthering Heights" Live vocal track. April 1978. (4 mins).

SECRET POLICEMAN'S THIRD BALL (UK)
"Running Up That Hill" (live with Dave Gilmour). March 1987. (5 mins).

SEIKO WATCH COMMERCIAL (JAPAN)
June 1978. (1 min).

SENSUAL WORLD OF KATE BUSH (USA)
Documentary with interview and video clips. Taped Nov 1989, aired Dec 1989. (25 mins).

SHOW VOR 8 (GERMANY)
"Running Up That Hill". (Del version). November 1985. (4 mins).

SKY CHANNEL (UK)
News clips of inauguration of new Satellite network. January 1984. (4 mins).

SOUNDS IN S (JAPAN)
Interview and video clips, including live versions of "the Long And Winding Road", "She's Leaving Home" and "Let It Be". June 1978. (14 mins).

SWEDISH TV SPECIAL 1979
37 min

TISWAS (UK)
4/14/79 3 min

TOP OF THE POPS (UK)
"And So Is Love" 17 Nov, 1994

TOP OF THE POPS (UK)
"Hounds Of Love" 3 March 1986 (4 mins).

TOP OF THE POPS (UK)
"Running Up That Hill" (grey suits version).22 August 1985. (4 mins).

TOP POP (GERMANY)
"Wuthering Heights" Apr 1978. (4 mins).

TUBE (UK)
"Under The Ivy" live at Abbey Road Studio 19 March 1986 (3 mins).

WINTER SNOWTIME SPECIAL (UK)
"December Will Be Magic Again". Different audio mix. 12 December 1979. (4 mins).

WOGAN (UK)
"Experiment IV" . 31 October 1986. (5 mins).

WOGAN (UK)
"Running Up That Hill" August 1985 different version (4 mins).

WOGAN 12/16/91
(Rocket Man) 5 min

Y. NOAH (FRANCE)
"Suspended In Gaffa" (black dress version). October 1982. (4 mins).

ZIM ZUM ZAM (ITALY)
"The Dreaming" (green light version). September 1982. (5 mins).

Peter Gabriel & Kate Bush Singles

Don't Give Up / In Your Eyes
Virgin PGS 2 (UK)
Virgin PGSP 2 (UK) fold poster sleeve.
Virgin 505441 (Portugal)

Don't Give Up/ In Your Eyes (Special Mix)
Virgin PGS 2 (UK)
Virgin 108 289 (Germany)
Charisma 108.289 (Spain)

Don't Give Up/ Sledgehammer
Virgin 25853 (Argentina)

Don't Give Up / Curtains
Geffen 728463 (US)

Don't Give Up/ In Your Eyes - This Is The Picture
Virgin 608 289 213 (Gmy & Spain) 12"

Don't Give Up/ Don't Give Up - Curtains
Geffen 20645OA (US) 12"

Don't Give Up/ In Your Eyes – This is the Picture
Virgin PGS 212B (Australia) 12"

Don't Give Up/ In Your Eyes
Virgin PGS 23 (Australia) 7"

GUEST APPEARANCES

(alphabetical by artist and title)

1986 Out Now
EMI HPP 260851 (Australia) compilation featuring 'Running Up That Hill'

20 With A Bullet
EMI EMTV 32 (UK) Compilation featuring 'Sat In Your Lap'

Always & Forever
Featuring 'The Man With The Child In His Eyes'

Best Of British Pop Music
STARCD 3313 (Holland) featuring 'The Wedding List' also UK vinyl STAR 2275

Best Of Celtic
Warner Music 5050466-5329-5 Mná na hÉireann

Best Of Love
EMI538 361 2 Hounds Of Love

Big Country The Seer
Phonogram MERH 87 (UK), 826844 1 Vertigo Polygram (US)

Bitter Suites
EMI - CDLIC70 (UK) Came free with Sunday Times newspaper The Man With The Child In His Eyes

British Invasion
EMS-91137 (Japan) Running Up That Hill

Castaway Movie Soundtrack
EMC 3529 (UK) Featuring 'Be Kind To My Mistakes'

Celtic Circle - Celtic Mystery Album
BMG Poland, 7432 198812 Women Of Ireland

Celtic Heartbeat Collection 2
UD 53122 CD Mná na hÉireann

Christmas Megastars
EMI 543 700-2 December Will Be Magic Again

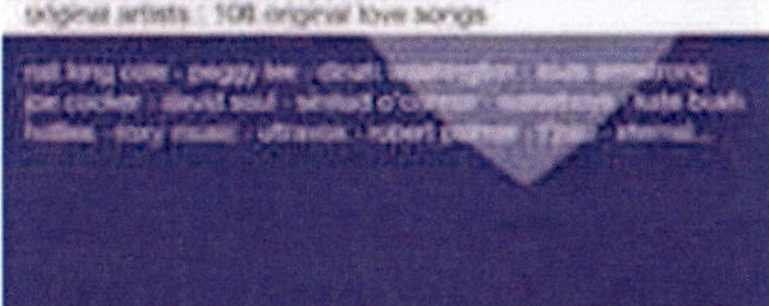

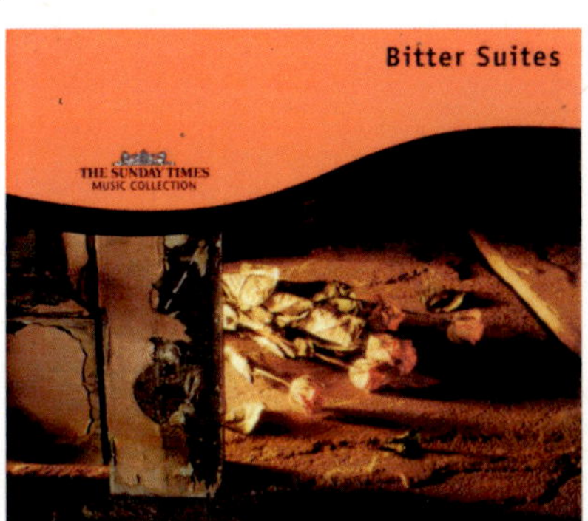

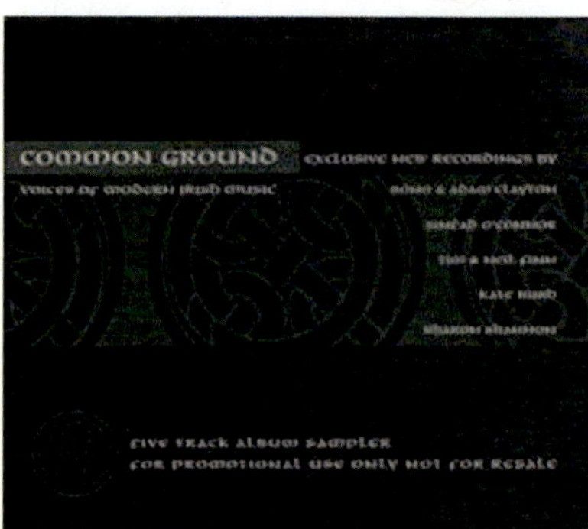

Common Ground
EMI Premier E2-37691 (USA) Mna Na H-Eireann

Common Ground Sampler
EMI Premier - CDAS 110 (Holland) Mna Na H-Eireann

Earthrise
POLYDOR - 515 587-2 (Canada) Don't Give Up (Peter Gabriel & Kate Bush)

Earthrise
Polygram - EARTH 1 (UK) Sampler Don't Give Up (Peter Gabriel & Kate Bush)

Edge Of Christmas
Oglio Collection 581 585-2 December Will Be Magic Again

Felicity
Hollywood 162 228-2 This Woman's Work

Ferry Aid - Let it Be
AID 1 UK 7" featuring Kate

Ferry Aid - Let It Be
AID T1 Sun Records (UK) 12"

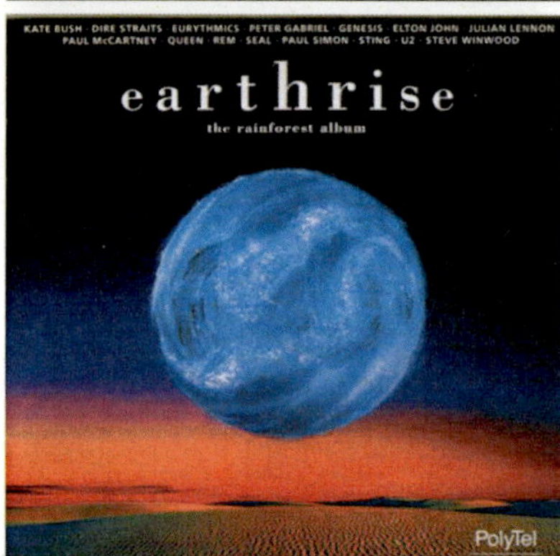

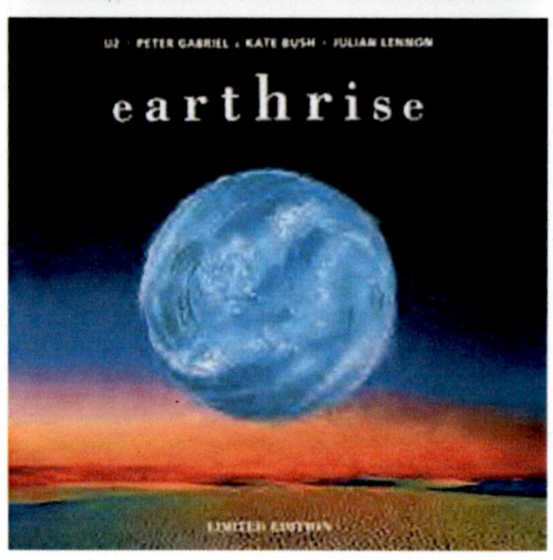

Glory Of Gershwin
Mercury5260912 CD (UK) The Man I Love

Go West - Dancing On the Couch
Chrysalis BHV 41550

Go West - The King Is Dead
Chrysalis GOW 6 (UK) 7"

Grand Theft Auto Vice City Vol 3
Sony includes "Wow"

Greatest Love
EMI 5955802 Man With The Child In His Eyes

Greatest Hits Of The 80s
EMI5710962 Babooshka

Greatest Hits Of The 90s
EMI5711002, Rubberband Girl

Greatest Love
Featuring 'Wuthering Heights'

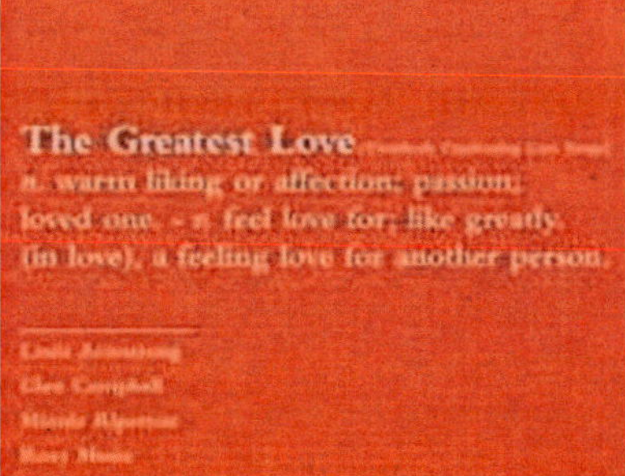

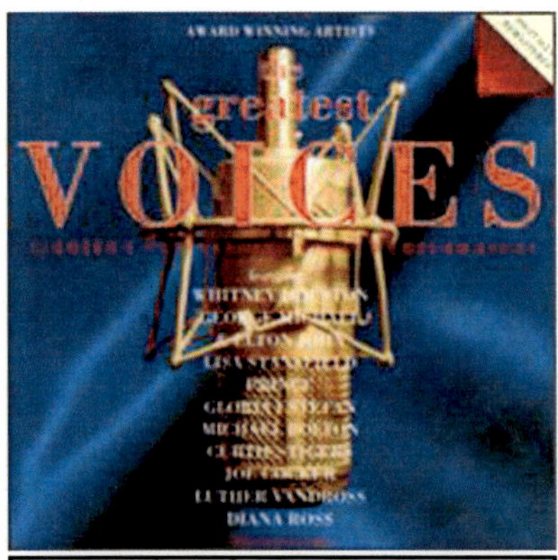

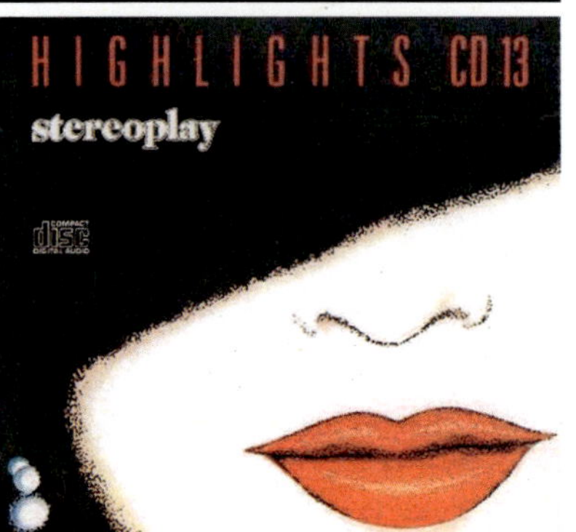

Greatest Voices
Dino 44 CD Running Up That Hill

Greenpeace
DATE 827 351 2 'Breathing'

Greenpeace Album
Tower Bell FUND 1 (UK), A & M SP 5091 (US), Featuring 'Breathing'

Highlights
Ariole Eurodisc CD607 809 (Germany) Cloudbusting

Hits Hits Hits 5
Featuring 'Hounds Of Love'

Hits Of The 70's
Featuring 'Wuthering Heights'
Reader's Digest 6LP set

It's Christmas
CDEMTV 49 (UK) compilation featuring a completely different version of 'December Will Be Magic'

It's Christmas
EMTV 49(UK) compilation with completely different version of 'December Will Be Magic'

Let's Hear It For The Girls
Featuring 'Cloudbusting'

Lista Przebojów Programu III - 1986
Pomaton EMI, 497 624 2 Cloudbusting

Lista Przebojów Programu III - 1988
Pomaton EMI, 499 123 2 Sisters & Brothers (Midge Ure & Kate Bush)

Lista Przebojów Programu III - 1989
Pomaton EMI, 499 124 2 The Sensual World

LIVING IN OBLIVION The 80's Greatest Hits Volume 2
EMI, E2-89605 Running Up That Hill

Michael Kamen Soundtrack Album
LONDON 458 912-2 Brazil (new version)

Midge Ure Answers To Nothing
Chrysalis FV41649

Mid-Price Hits
EMI(Denmark) Magazine give-away Running Up That Hill

Movies Of My Dreams
Warner Music Poland, 5046-71250-2 Sam Lowry's Dream/Brazil

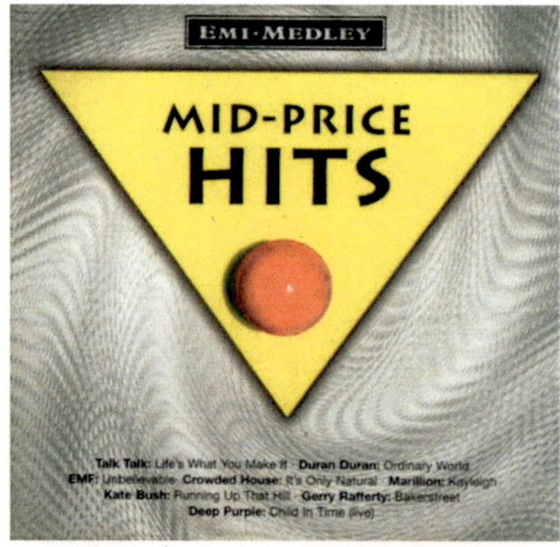

MTV Closet Classics
CBS LP462927 1 (Australia) compilation featuring 'Wuthering Heights'

Music Of The Millenium
Universal Music - Millenium3 - 1 (Spain) Sampler Pic 197 Don't Give Up (Peter Gabriel & Kate Bush)

Now That's What I Call Music 10
Featuring 'Don't Give Up'

Now That's What I Call Music 8
Featuring Running Up That Hill

Ongoing History of New Music
EMI/ (Canada) Wuthering Heights

Original 80's Album
Pomaton EMI, 582 564 2 Babooshka

Paramount Pictures 90th Anniversary Memorable Songs Legacy 1CK86827 (USA) This Woman's Work

Peter Gabriel - Games Without Frontiers
Charisma CB 354 (UK) 7"

Peter Gabriel - No Self Control
Charisma CB 360 (UK) 7"

Peter Gabriel - Peter Gabriel III
Charisma CDS 4019 (UK),
Charisma/Polygram CA 12215 (US)

Peter Gabriel - Peter Gabriel
Geffen 92035 2 (US), Virgin PGCD 3 (UK), Virgin XCDSCD 4019 (UK) Sung in German, Virgin 250929 (Germany), Virgin 256954 (Germany) Sung in German, Virgin JPN VJCP 2331 (Japan) Features Kate on backing vocals on 'Games Without Frontiers', and 'No Self Control'.

Peter Gabriel - Shaking The Tree: Sixteen Golden Greats
Geffen 493 274-2 Don't Give Up Games Without Frontiers

Peter Gabriel - So
Charisma Virgin PG5 (UK), Geffen 9 24088 1 (US)Featuring Don't Give Up

Peter Gabriel - So
Geffen 924088 2 (US), Charisma PGCD 5 (UK), Virgin 257587 (Germany), Virgin JPN VJCP 2333 (Japan), WEA CD 24088 (Canada)
Features Kate duet with Gabriel on 'Don't Give Up'

Peter Gabriel Hit
EMI, 595 237-2 Don't Give Up, Games Without Frontiers, No Self Control

Platinum 80's
Warner Music, 0927-40968-2 Babooshka

Pop Classics - 28 Classic Tracks

Prince's Trust Collection
Telstar STAR 2275 (UK) Double album, featuring 'The Wedding List'

Q - The Album
Telstar CD1 TCD 2522 (UK) Features 'This Woman's Work'.

Q - The Album
Telstar STAR 2522 (UK) Features 'This Woman's Work'

Ray Shell - Them Heavy People
EMI 5142 (UK) 7"

Retro 80's Volume 1
EMI, 94887 (UK) Running Up That Hill (12" Mix)

Roy Harper - Once
Awareness AWCD 1018 (UK)
Awareness AWL 1018

Roy Harper Hats Off
Capitol 27640 You

Roy Harper The Unknown Soldier
SHVL 820 (UK)

Secret Policeman's Third Ball The Music
Virgin CDV 2458 Benefit album featuring Kate doing 'Running Up That Hill' live with Dave Gilmour.

Secret's Policeman's Third Ball
Virgin 1 90643 (US), Virgin V2458 (UK) Featuring 'Running Up That Hill' Live with Dave Gilmour

She's Having A Baby Soundtrack
IRS HUGHES IRSD 6211 (US) Featuring a different mix of 'This Woman's Work'

She's Having A Baby Soundtrack
IRS 6211 (US) Featuring different mix of 'This Woman's Work'

Sing Children Sing / Rainbow Games
CBS 8061 (UK) Lesley Duncan charity single with Kate and Paddy pictured on the cover and singing in the chorus.

Spinning Pups
EMI SF17099 (Canada) Compilation featuring 'Man With The Child In His Eyes'

Spirit Of The Forest
Virgin 796551 0 (US) 12"

Spirit Of The Forest
VS 1191 (UK) 7" featuring Kate and other guest stars

Stars Explosion
K-Tel, TI159 Babooshka

Tell It Through The Song
TELLEDISC (UK) Mail order only triple album featuring 'Man With The Child In His Eyes'

Theodore: An Alternative Music Sampler
Epic 446 062-2 Be Kind To My Mistakes (Edited Remix)

Ultimate British Collection
Quality QRSP 1040 (Canada) Compilation featuring 'The Wedding List'

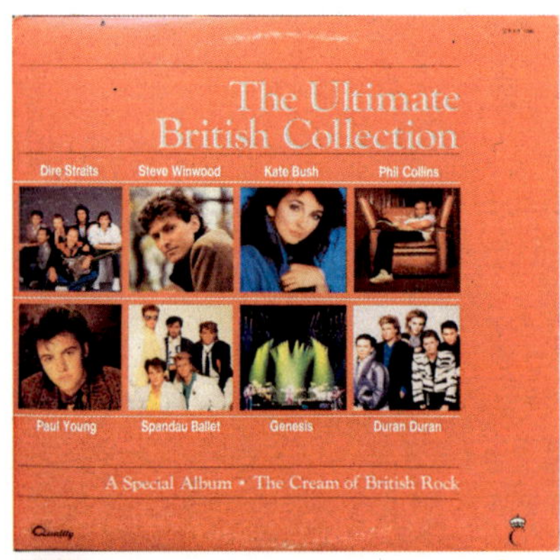

Utterly Utterly Live - Comic Relief
WEA WX 51 (UK) WEA 240932 1 (New Zealand)Featuring 'Do Bears...' and 'Breathing'

Wonderful Box 80's
BMG Poland, 7432 188153 2 Running Up That Hill

Wonderful Christmas Time
Toshiba EMI (Japan) featuring 'December Will Be Magic'

Zaine Griff - Figures
Polydor POLO 5061

Zaine Griff - Flowers
Polydor POSP 506 7" from above album

KATE IN PRINT

Words & Music from The Kick Inside
EMI Music Publishing (1978). Featuring Kite, Moving, The Kick Inside, Saxophone Song, Wuthering Heights, James & the Cold Gun, The Man With The Child In His Eyes ISBN: 095050565X

Wuthering Heights
EMI Music Publishing (1978). Sheet music.

The Man With The Child In His Eyes
EMI Music Publishing (1978). Sheet music.

Them Heavy People
EMI Music Publishing (1979). Sheet music.

Lionheart
EMI Music Publishing (1979). Featuring the entire music and lyrics for the second album. ISBN: 0861750101

Wow
EMI Music Publishing (1979). Sheet music.

Hammer Horror
EMI Music Publishing (1979). Sheet music.

December Will Be Magic Again
EMI Music Publishing (1980). Sheet music.

Babooshka
EMI Music Publishing (1980). Sheet music.

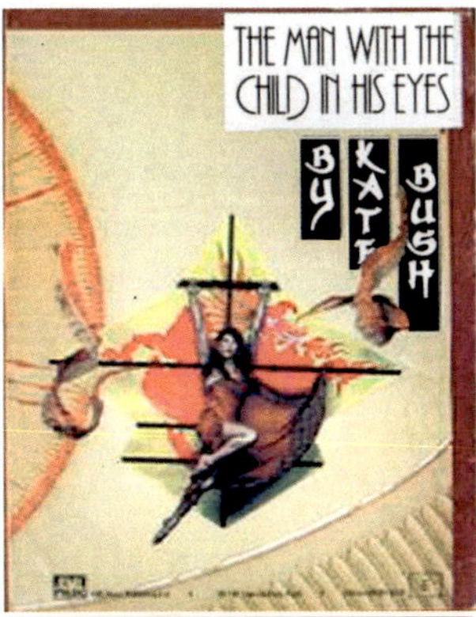

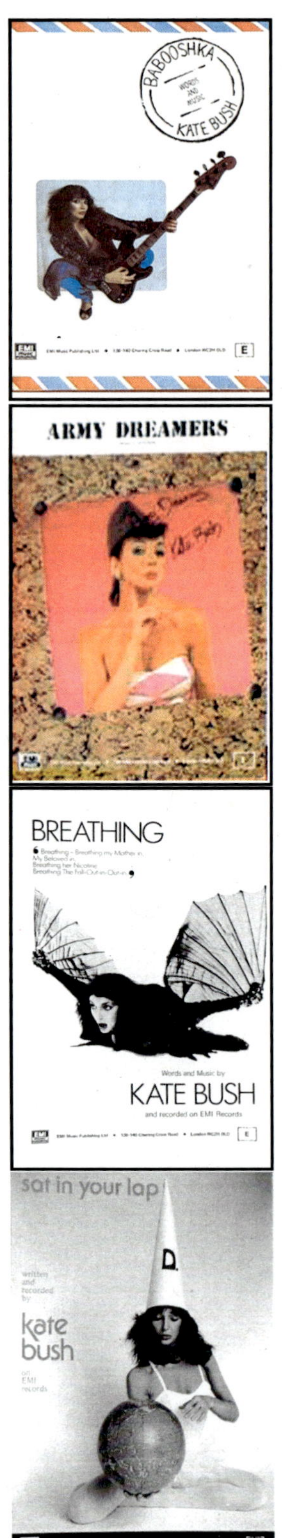

Army Dreamers
EMI Music Publishing (1980). Sheet music.

Breathing
EMI Music Publishing (1980). Sheet music.

Sat In Your Lap
EMI Music Publishing (1981). Sheet music.

The Best Of Kate Bush
EMI Music Publishing (1981). Featuring music and lyrics from thirteen songs with remarks by Kate. ISBN 0861751639

Hounds Of Love
EMI Music Publishing (1985). Featuring music and lyrics to the entire album and a fold out poster.

Running Up That Hill
EMI Music Publishing (1985). Sheet music. Also Castle Music PTY Australia

Cloudbusting
EMI Music Publishing (1985). Sheet music.

Hounds Of Love
EMI Music Publishing (1985). Sheet music. ISBN: 0861753658

The Big Sky
EMI Music Publishing (1985). Sheet music.

Experiment IV
EMI Music Publishing (1986). Sheet music.

The Whole Story
EMI Music Publishing (1986). Song book with the entire album. Also Warner USA ISBN: 0861754107

Complete
EMI Music Publishing/ International Music Publications (1987).
Music and lyrics to 66 songs, also an abridged discography and videography.

Kate Bush
International Music Publications (1987) Music and lyrics to eight songs with guitar boxes. ISBN 1859094457

The Sensual World
EMI Music Publishing ISBN: 0863596827

The Red Shoes Songbook
EMI Music Publishing ISBN 185909158X

Rubberband Girl
EMI Music Publishing 18790 Sheet Music

With Love
An unauthorised compilation of news clippings covering Kate's career up to 1985. Because this was essentially violating dozens of copyrights, it is no surprise that there is no credit for the compiler or publishing company. An extremely convenient way to acquire a lot of interesting articles.

The Secret History Of Kate Bush
Omnibus Press (1983). Controversial semi biography by Fred Vermorel.

Biography - Princess Of Suburbia
Target (1980). Illustrated Biography by Fred & Judy Vermorel.

Kate Bush - An Illustrated Biography
Proteus (1980). By Paul Kerton.

Cathy
Kindlight-Kent (1986)
Westerham Press. Beautiful book of 32 pictures of Kate as a child, taken by her brother. Very limited edition.

A Visual Documentary
Omnibus Press (1988). Day by day look at Kate's career fully illustrated. By Kevin Cann & Sean Mayes.

The Whole Story
Sidgwick & Jackson (1988). Illustrated biography by Kerry Juby.

Kate Bush Collection Off The Record
EMI Music ISBN 1859091695

Waiting For Kate Bush
Omnibus John Mendelssohn
ISBN 1844494896

Kate Bush I Segugi dell'Amore
Monica Tessarin 88-7255-225-7

The Complete Kate Bush
EMI Music Publishing Song Book

Kate Bush The Biography
Rob Jovanovic 0749950498

Programmes

The Tour of Life concert programme is perhaps one of the most desirable collectibles to the Kate Bush collector. Beautifully packaged in a full colour folder, with a set of three postcards, a couple of sheets of what is presumably writing paper, an application form to join the Fan Club, and a letter from Nicholas Wade, the fan club secretary. The ony other concert programme is from the Bill Duffield charity concert, it is not as attractive but is obviously rarer.

FANZINES & WWW

During the 1980's and 90's there were a wealth of fanzines from around the world. The official one from "The Kate Bush Club" in the UK has been appearing sporadically since 1979, they are not numbered. Many of these publications still exist as websites.

Popular websites include:

www.gaffa.org
www.katebushnews.com
www.geocities.com/SunsetStrip/Palms/1730/
www.geocities.com/etherealworldofkatebush/
www.paradiseplace.org.uk/Kate/index.htm
www.katebush.cjb.net/
www.antenna.nl/~dinyar/
www.katebushforum.com

The official website is www.katebush.com.

DVD

Kate Bush has been in the vanguard of the music video revolution since its beginning which makes it all the more surprising that there are so few Kate Bush DVDs available. Presumably this oversight will be corrected in the months ahead with the release of Aerial.

The Greatest Hits 4929839 EMI Records (UK) The Man With The Child In His Eyes

The Secret Policeman's Ball - The Complete Edition Int. Licensing and Copyright Ltd DVD2254

The Hit Collection Synergie Logistics MDV068 Wuthering Heights

The Greatest Love EMI Records (UK) 4929819

Two Rooms: Celebrating the Songs of Elton John & Bernie Taupin (1991) (Brazil) Super D / Phantom So. Possibly twodifferent covers for this.

Kate Bush:The Line the Cross & The Curve (1999) Sony Music (USA) I haven't actually seen this but it is said to exist!

Duran Duran - The Secret Policeman's Third Ball Sono Press (Brazil)

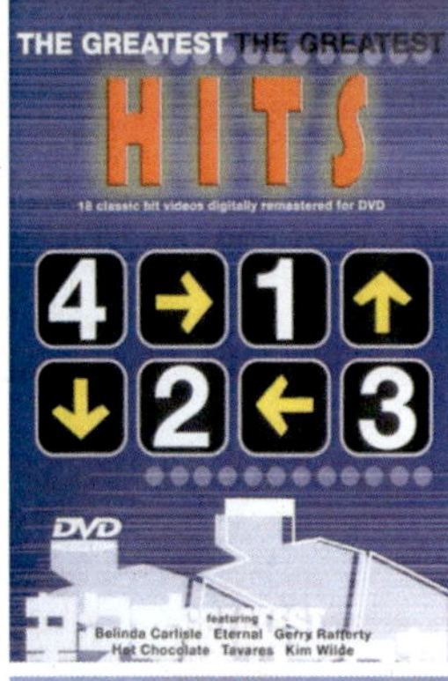

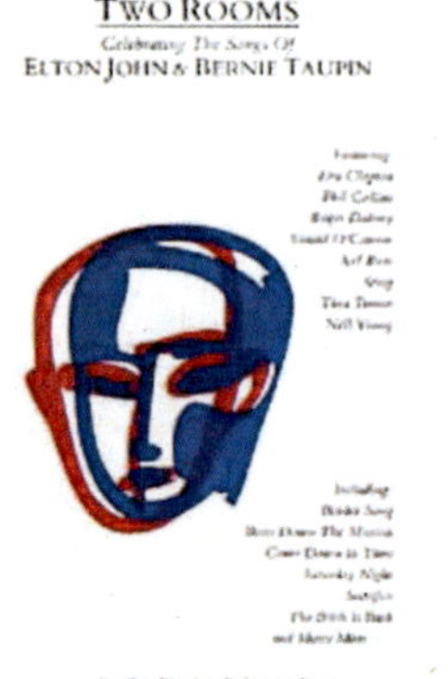